POSTMODERNISM

Postmodernism

Kevin O'Donnell

LION
ACCESS
GUIDES

Copyright © 2003 Kevin O'Donnell
This edition copyright © 2003 Lion
Publishing

The author asserts the moral right
to be identified as the author of this work

Published by
Lion Publishing plc
Mayfield House, 256 Banbury Road,
Oxford OX2 7DH, England
www.lion-publishing.co.uk
ISBN 0 7459 5092 2

First edition 2003
10 9 8 7 6 5 4 3 2 1 0

All rights reserved

A catalogue record for this book is
available from the British Library

Typeset in 10.25/11 Venetian 301
Printed and bound in China

Text acknowledgments
p. 6: extract from 'On a New Work in the English
Tongue' from *Electric Light* by Seamus Heaney, copyright
© 2001 Seamus Heaney, published by Faber and Faber
Ltd. Reproduced by permission of Faber and Faber Ltd
(UK), and Farrar, Straus and Giroux, LLC (USA).

Scripture quotations taken from the *Holy Bible, New
International Version*, copyright © 1973, 1978, 1984
International Bible Society. Used by permission of
Zondervan and Hodder & Stoughton Limited. All
rights reserved. The 'NIV' and 'New International
Version' trademarks are registered in the United
States Patent and Trademark Office by International
Bible Society. Use of either trademark requires the
permission of International Bible Society. UK
trademark number 1448790.

Picture acknowledgments
Please see page 160.

Contents

Note
Throughout this series the convention is followed of dating events by the abbreviations BCE (Before Common Era) and CE (Common Era). They correspond precisely to the more familiar BC and AD.

Introducing Postmodernism

'Post' means 'after' and 'modern' is 'up to date' or 'now'. Thus, the term 'postmodern' could be translated as 'beyond the now'. What does it mean, or feel like, to be 'beyond the now'? It is fast, on the go, ever-changing, just like life. It flows. To be 'beyond the now' is to live on the edge. This sounds rather Zen-like, and that is not far from the mark. Postmodernism is concerned with non-linear, expressive and supra-rational discourses that have been marginalized and atrophied under the influence of the Enlightenment. To explore the postmodern is to explore ourselves again and to link up with a partially forgotten past.

'Postmodernism' is the name given to a range of philosophical positions and aesthetic styles that have developed since the 1950s. It is a diverse movement with some conflicting opinions, but the term coheres as it describes several dominant features.

Post-this, post-that, post-the-other, yet in the end
Not past a thing. Not understanding or telling
or forgiveness.
But often past oneself,
Pounded like a shore by the roller griefs
In language that can still knock language sideways.
SEAMUS HEANEY,
'ON A NEW WORK IN THE ENGLISH TONGUE'

Underlying everything is the belief that all human knowledge is limited and culturally conditioned: each age thinks in a certain way; humanity cannot help it. As a result, there is no way to escape language, no way to stand outside discourse to get at pure, raw truth. So, is there a place for absolutes and constants in this scheme of things, and, indeed, what future is there for revealed religious faiths?

In this discussion, it will be necessary to outline earlier philosophical ideas and movements to show how and why postmodernism has developed, and what it is reacting to. Not

every philosopher mentioned in this book will actually be a postmodernist – some who are usually counted as such never used that title. Postmodernism is a movement that developed after the Second World War, but some earlier philosophers taught ideas that link up with postmodernism, or provided seed thoughts that were developed further. Postmodernism was not born in a conceptual vacuum. It has a prehistory.

The following chapters guide the reader through the history and basic ideas of postmodernism, introducing some key thinkers along the way. The last spread in each chapter includes a brief summary of the key theme of the chapter as a whole. There are, inescapably, many technical terms in a book like this, and these are explained in the Rapid Factfinder at the end of the book. There is also an Index of Key Thinkers (with a guide to their main publications), which will help you look them up quickly and easily.

BEGINNING POSTMODERNISM

The term 'postmodernism' was first used by artists in the late 19th and early 20th centuries to denote new movements that were breaking free of an old order. The term quickly spread to other disciplines.

In 1975, Charles Jenks wrote *The Language of Post-Modern Architecture*. In this narrow field, he defined a key element of the postmodern condition: modernist simplification, minimalism and universalizing styles were reworked

The Humboldt Library in Berlin, which was designed by Charles Moore (1925–93).

with more decoration. Different styles and periods were mixed quite deliberately, even ironically. Architects no longer believed in one, dominant style. They were no longer of their time, but seemed to step beyond it and see all previous styles as accessible.

It was also in the 1970s that continental postmodern philosophers became popular in the USA and the term thundered ahead into popular usage. But what is 'post' and what is 'modern'? All the 'posts' we hear about are partly defined by what came before

— they are dependent on and reacting against an earlier movement. Thus, we cannot understand postmodernism without first looking at modernism. Modernism, in turn, derived from earlier movements that made new discoveries or rediscovered old knowledge. So, to understand postmodernism, we must trace its ancestry back through history and see what it is reacting against.

Contents

Our working hypothesis is that the status of knowledge is altered as societies enter what is known as the post-industrial age and cultures enter what is known as the postmodern age. This transition has been under way since at least the end of the 1950s, which for Europe marks the completion of reconstruction...

JEAN-FRANÇOIS LYOTARD,
THE POSTMODERN CONDITION

The Renaissance and After

Philosophy developed from the Middle Ages to the Enlightenment, with the role of reason gradually becoming paramount.

The medieval world had largely lost sight of much older, classical learning. Texts were kept in monasteries, and only a few people were sufficiently educated to read and copy them. However, new trade routes to the East meant the discovery of old documents long lost to the West, some in Greek, some translated into Arabic or Syriac. The ancient wisdom of Greeks such as Plato (427–347 BCE) and Aristotle (384–322 BCE) had sometimes been preserved in Muslim societies. This led to a rebirth of learning – 'the Renaissance' – which had its effects from the 14th to 16th centuries. It was not exactly a reassertion of the power of

reason, for many Renaissance thinkers were obsessed with occult arts such as alchemy, or saw nature as a sacred system of signs.

The Scholastics

Until the Renaissance, the church held sway in the intellectual world. The Scholastics, learned monks and theologians, the most prominent of whom was Thomas Aquinas (c. 1225–74), fused the views of Greek philosophy (particularly Aristotle) to Christian theology. This system developed from the 5th century to the 13th century, and was seen by the church as sufficient for all time. What the ancients had not revealed about nature and the world was beyond mortal ken! New ideas were considered subversive and dangerous, and some had to be smuggled into the public domain in the guise of commentaries and footnotes on existing texts.

Modern philosophy emerged as thinkers such as René Descartes (1596–1650) challenged this world view and intellectual control. A sceptical, rational mood arose, which gave birth to logical analysis and the scientific method. At that time, science was not a

The occult view of nature led to amusing parallels between the shape of an item and its power or purpose. Ingesting a phallus-shaped root, for example, was thought to cure sexual impotence.

The church guarded all learning in the medieval period. Eleventh-century manuscript illlumination by Pope Urban II, depicting the consecration of the Benedictine abbey at Cluny, France.

[Descartes] is best known, perhaps, as the man who said, 'Cogito, ergo sum' — 'I am thinking, therefore I am.' This little piece of reasoning is the first principle of his metaphysics or first philosophy, his theory of what has to be known for stable or exact science to be possible at all.

TOM SORRELL,
*DESCARTES: A VERY SHORT
INTRODUCTION*

separate discipline, but merely part of philosophy.

The Enlightenment

The Enlightenment was the name given to a movement stretching from the 17th to the 18th centuries, in which reason reigned supreme and war was waged against superstition. This drive brought greater demands for tolerance, for more democratic government, the concept of the innate rights of man (witness Thomas Paine's work in the newly independent USA), and scientific discovery after discovery. No longer were scholars content to take the past masters at their word. They went out and observed things for themselves, experimenting and cataloguing.

You Can't Stop Progress?

The Enlightenment led to reason and the scientific method emerging triumphant over faith and the church, but at what cost?

The Enlightenment saw the birth of autonomous scientific method. Underlying this method was the belief that the more we followed reason, the more we would progress. There were great technological leaps forward with every new invention. The harnessing of steam power and the consequent growth of factories and railways revolutionized production and transport. Ships were not just dependent upon the wind. Electricity further changed the world, and allowed rapid advancements in communications and media in the years ahead.

The *Titanic* was perhaps the pinnacle of the triumphant march of science. The incessant momentum and belief in human progress and the power of reason to control nature peaked in this project. This 'unsinkable' ship was a marvel

FRIEDRICH NIETZSCHE

The German philosopher Friedrich Nietzche (1844–1900) was a subversive, iconoclastic thinker well in advance of his time. He criticized philosophy for idolizing reason at the expense of the emotions. He saw the 4th-century BCE Greek philosopher Socrates as the main culprit. Socrates had equated reason with virtue and thus with happiness. Nietzsche theorized that emphasizing reason alone suppresses many of the other components that make us human beings: philosophers were analysing and classifying like museum curators, and sought the real in the abstract. It was like handling conceptual mummies; they were 'Egypticizing' thought. Something had gone astray, in the name of reason and human liberation.

The *Titanic*, 1912 – a great technological achievement that was boasted to be 'unsinkable'. Sadly, it was not, and this shocked and dented belief in the inevitability of progress.

of human engineering, and yet it sank with tragic loss of life in 1912 on its maiden voyage. Shortly afterwards, the First World War scattered the benign hopes of a rational, tolerant, emancipated future for all. Darkness and savagery still lived in human hearts.

The Industrial Revolution had brought new commodities and wealth, but at what expense? Traditional communities had been destroyed, and the environment polluted.

All that philosophers have been handling for thousands of years is conceptual mummies; nothing real has ever left their hands.

FRIEDRICH NIETZSCHE,
TWILIGHT OF THE IDOLS

13

Modernism

Modernism was a mixture of Enlightenment values and the emerging postmodern emphasis on mixing styles, self-awareness and the poetic.

Enlightenment values were shaken up in the early part of the 20th century with the advent of the 'modernists'. Modernism as a movement stretches from about 1910 until the outbreak of the Second World War. Modernists were scientific disciples, hoping for a brave, new world, and utilizing technology and mathematics in their designs. They were beginning to question the old order and left it shattered in their wake.

New literary forms

Writers tried a new, disjointed style, breaking up the narrative flow and using many different genres – poetry, letter writing, prose, stream of consciousness – to suggest and symbolize the break-up of the old world order. James Joyce's *Ulysses* and T.S. Eliot's *The Waste Land* (both published in 1922) are prime examples. There was an attempt and a desire to see how reality could be portrayed, rather than seeking to replicate nature like the human eye and the camera. Questions of interpretation and point of view were now being considered.

Technology and subversion

Modernism is a blend of several forces. There was still belief in science and technology as the world spun with new inventions – the telephone, the wireless,

ART AND ARCHITECTURE

The world of art saw the birth of new movements – cubism, dadaism, surrealism and futurism. No longer were artists portraying reality slavishly and photographically. Images were exploded, figures ignored the rules of perspective, and colours were used with a disregard for nature and light.

New movements in architecture were minimalist, stripping decoration down to the basics, seeking geometrical designs and harmonies, and a universal style across nations. Cubism could play with geometry too, but the surrealists plumbed the subconscious and let the imagination flow.

Artists of the futurist movement sought to portray the dazzling speed and colour of modern city life in their work. *The City Rises* (1910–11) by Umberto Boccioni (1882–1916).

> *Modernism tore up unity and postmodernism has been enjoying the shreds.*
>
> TODD GITLIN,
> *CULTURAL POLITICS IN CONTEMPORARY AMERICA*

commercial flight, electric lighting and household appliances – but at the same time, the old confidence was dying and voices of protest were being raised. It has been pointed out (for example, by critics such as Jurgen Habermas) that these more radical attitudes are akin to postmodern thought. It is the same spirit at play. Postmodernism should not be seen, then, as a distinctly chronological movement, but an outlook that can occur in different ages. But while modernism grieves the breakdown of unity and the old order of reason, postmodernism celebrates the resulting diversity and lack of centre.

Narratives of Emancipation

Great hopes were held for human liberation, progress and social change. These ended in disillusionment with the advent of the Second World War.

Modernism embraced new technologies and the hope that science could help to make a better world. There was a shake up of ideas after the First World War, but there was still hope. Europe was fired by theories of social emancipation. The grand narratives of utopian socialism and Marxism gained a boost when the Tsar of Russia was overthrown and the Bolshevik revolution created the first communist state. The atmosphere was electric, and governments feared uprisings across Europe.

Struggles abounded between the left and the right as fascism arose in Spain, Italy and Germany. This form of dictatorial rule tried to preserve features of the old order, and pandered to baser human instincts such as racism. The Spanish Civil War in the 1930s was a testing ground for the commitment of both sides. Both were idealistic, and Germany could have gone one way or the other in the Depression that followed the First World War.

A spectre is haunting Europe, the spectre of communism…

KARL MARX,
THE COMMUNIST
MANIFESTO

Disillusionment

The narratives of emancipation had their roots in Christian eschatology (the study of the last things); Karl Marx's notion that a working-class revolution was inevitable was as much an act of faith as a sound economic and philosophical analysis. These ideals were dealt a crushing blow with the outbreak of the Second World War and the atrocities that could be perpetrated by left and right (Stalin's purges and gulags; Hitler's Holocaust).

The post-war period was one of economic growth for the West and stagnation for the East. The cold war dominated politics, symbolized by the Berlin Wall. The two superpowers of the USA and the USSR faced each other off, each claiming to be the virtuous party. Politics stagnated into

'Long live the fifth anniversary of the Great Proletarian Revolution!' Poster by Ivan Simakov, 1922. Marxism gained political power amid hopes that widespread social revolution and emancipation would follow. Marx believed the proletariat, or working class, would rise up against capitalism, leading to a classless society.

capitalist consumerism and communist dictatorship. It was only a matter of time before the Communist Bloc imploded under economic pressure and a grass-roots demand for reform. Eventually, the Berlin Wall came down, but in China the Tiananmen Square protestors were brutally suppressed. Communism disintegrated as people washed their hands of it, or it was kept alive by bullets and tanks.

With hopes dashed, and the emancipation narratives in tatters, what would fill the vacuum?

17

Consumer Philosophy?

Technology that had been developed to fight wars was adapted for consumer use in peacetime, resulting in rapid social change.

The developed world saw a further explosion of technology after the Second World War as nations rebuilt their economies and inventions flourished. TV brought the world closer, creating a 'global village', in the words of Marshall McLuhan. Computers that had been expensive and bulky came into many homes with the silicon revolution. The internet – originally a military tool – links people up even more with emails that can whizz across the globe in minutes.

The medium is the message.

MARSHALL McLUHAN, UNDERSTANDING MEDIA

Increased prosperity has led to greater consumer spending. The media (with satellite TV, videos, DVDs, CDs and so forth), the creation of youth culture to target fashion labels and musical styles, and the development of information technology (with palmtops, digital cameras, mobile phones and… what next?) has created a fast-paced, multilayered, many-messaged society. It is spreading a way of life, a set of expectations, and the same images, logos and products, swallowing local culture in its wake.

Cultural soup

One aspect of postmodernism is the constantly shifting information overload as ideologies compete in the marketplace. Styles and ideas from different ages, and from across the globe, are accessible and at play in a vast soup of signs. Life has become faster, more decentred, with shifting values and uncertain hopes.

A post-industrial fad?

Fredric Jameson, a Marxist cultural critic, has written a critique of postmodernism (*Postmodernism, or the Cultural Logic of Late Capitalism*), seeing it as a socially conditioned passing fad. It is appropriate, he says, for the late 20th and early 21st century, but will give way to newer patterns of thought. He traces changes in

As landmarks go, the golden arches of McDonald's can be seen the world over. It is said that they are more familiar than the Christian cross.

Pop star Madonna reinvents her image constantly, mixing fashions, eras, cultures and styles. She has been described as the perfect postmodern icon.

thinking after 1848 (with market capitalism, early steam power and machinery) to the rise of monopoly capitalism after 1890 (with electricity and combustion engines). Changes continue, and the postmodern condition comes in the wake of the changes after the Second World War, with more international communication and technology that creates multinational capitalism. According to Jameson, the clash of styles that forms postmodernism is found exactly in this consumer madness.

There is something in this analysis, but perhaps there is more at work than mere consumerism.

Sceptics

Is postmodernism a shallow, empty scepticism that rides on the crest of too many rapid social changes and does not have any bearings or anything useful to say?

Analysts such as Fredric Jameson seem to be borne out by the radical scepticism that some postmodern thought produces. Every type of knowledge is questioned; it is difficult to tell which way is up any more. Life and society become decentred; there is a marketplace of values, reasons and lifestyles on offer. As British rock group the Manic Street Preachers once put it, 'This is my truth, tell me yours.'

This scepticism does not go all the way through for every postmodern philosopher. Some are merely trying to get a thinking response, to challenge authorities and illusions we have set up. They are not necessarily denying that there is any

> Il n'y a pas de hors-texte.
> (*There is no outside-text.*)
>
> JACQUES DERRIDA, *OF GRAMMATOLOGY*

Human society tends to become more international and multi-ethnic, and has competing lifestyles on offer.

purpose or meaning to life. Some of postmodernism's key thinkers are very concerned with ethics and are involved in political movements. Questions of meaning and value have become more of an issue

Humans cannot step out of language, just as a fish cannot live out of water.

because of the views of language predominating in the 20th century.

The linguistic turn

Various schools of philosophy have converged on language. There has been a general agreement that meaning is to be found within language and not outside of human discourse. As human beings, we have to live within our discourse as fish live

in water. We cannot ever step outside the constraints of our language to experience reality in the raw. It is filtered, interpreted, through language. Our words do not merely refer to objects out there, but they are our creations, bearing an accidental relationship with the world. We impose order upon the world, and make 'worlds' from it. We impose meanings by our discourses. This is known as 'the linguistic turn'.

Some philosophers are very sceptical, seeing meaning as a human creation, free-floating and nothing to do with what is really real. Others see meaning as present only in logical statements that can be verified by sense experience or experimentation (the logical positivists). All else is meaningless.

Postmodern thinking has a place for emotion, though, seeing it as a vital part of human discourse. And maybe, just maybe, humans are responding to stimuli from around us, from 'out there', rather than totally creating values, order and meaning from scratch.

What Has Been Lost?

Materialism and consumerism have wrecked the environment and drained spirit and value from society. An almost exclusive stress on reason and progress has cost us dearly.

The triumph of reason led to a repression of the imaginative, the poetic, the symbolic and even the ethical, at times. Ancient ways of seeing the world perceived it as a place full of arcane wonder. Materialism has sought to bleed it dry, and has turned it into a commodity rather than a fragile but marvellous ecosystem (and our home). Hence pollution, global warming and many other ghastly scars have been inflicted upon our planet as we have tried to turn it into an object for pleasure.

Going back

Postmodernism has challenged the superiority of reason, following on from Nietzsche and the poet/artist William Blake in the 19th century. We need the emotions too.

Postmodern thinkers want to allow many different forms of discourse, many routes to knowledge – not just the rational. Seeing things from many sides helps to stop monopolization and spin-doctoring. Nietzsche warned that 'truth' was often someone's power. It was what people wanted you to believe.

There can be a space for the spiritual too in all of this exploration and honesty. Not all postmodern thinkers are radically sceptical and atheistic. Some are agnostic, open, and even want to believe.

Raw, unchecked reason has raped the planet.

Though some Christian churches decline, spirituality is high on the agenda of many non-Christians. There are numerous different spiritual paths on offer.

To see a World in a Grain of Sand,
And a Heaven in a Wild Flower,
Hold Infinity in the palm of
your hand
And Eternity in an Hour.

WILLIAM BLAKE,
'AUGURIES OF INNOCENCE'

You can't step into the same
river twice.

HERACLITUS (c. 500 BCE)

Humanity requires a holistic vision; scientific analysis is only one way of knowing, one string to the bow. Some postmodern thinkers are seeking out past ideas, polishing them up and making them their own, in a new context. It is not a simplistic about-turn, for postmoderns cannot be ancients. Too much has moved on and our perceptions are different.

Some thinkers seek out inspiration from the pre-Socratic, early Greek philosophers. Remember that it was Socrates, enshrined in Plato, who elevated reason (*logos*) above all other forms of discourse and knowledge. For him, even the most 'real' was sought in abstract terms. The pre-Socratics were more in tune with the wonder of the world, seeking to understand it, and having a place for mystic poetry too. Some postmodern philosophers write lyrically and playfully, in a non-linear manner.

23

Who Are the Postmodernists?

A 'rogues' gallery' of prominent postmodern thinkers follows. They do not all label themselves 'postmodernist', though; some call themselves 'post-structuralist'.

We are concerned with several key thinkers, and some others who influenced the postmodernism movement. It must be stressed that some of these men and women do not actually call themselves 'postmodernist'. Some refuse labels of any sort; others accept the term 'post-structuralist', reacting against structuralism, a particular strand of 20th-century thought. Their views are in accord with the postmodern condition, though, and other writers thus label them.

Roland Barthes (1915–80)

Barthes, a Frenchman, was an outsider to the French academic system for much of his life. He developed thought about signs (semiotics) and the roles and rules that we use for communication. His most famous text is *Mythologies*, a collection of short newspaper articles that reflect upon diverse images in society.

Jean Baudrillard (1929–)

The French philosopher Baudrillard has taken semiotics

Philosopher Roland Barthes.

– the study of the system of signs that we use – and analysed the forces that drive our society as those of consumerism. Money talks and all is image and hyper-reality. Who tells the truth, and did the Gulf War really happen, or was it a media-staged, virtual reality epic? Some key texts include *America*, *Seduction*, *The Illusion of the End* and *The Gulf War Did Not Take Place*.

> *A painful thought: past a certain point, history has not been real. Without realizing it, the whole human race seems to have suddenly left reality behind.*
>
> JEAN BAUDRILLARD,
> *FATAL STRATEGIES*

Gilles Deleuze (1925–95)

Deleuze was a far-ranging and eccentric thinker who was Professor of Philosophy at the University of Paris VIII, Vincennes. He wrote about literature and cinema, and raged against the anthropocentric view of the world in much philosophy, seeing human beings as a small part of a whole. He wondered at the way that we raise carbon-based life forms over silicon-based ones (flesh and blood versus artificial intelligence and computer chips). He speculates about machines, cybernetics and the future. It has been suggested that his work may have more significance in the 21st century as technology moves forward apace. Some key texts are the two-volume *Capitalism and Schizophrenia: Anti-Oedipus* and *A Thousand Plateaus*, on both of which he collaborated with another philosopher, Felix Guattari.

Jacques Derrida (1930–)

Derrida was born in Algiers, and at the age of 19 moved to France to study at École Normale Superieure. He developed ideas of studying philosophy as literature, and he has opened up philosophy and questioned many of its common assumptions. In his

Right: post-structuralist thinker Jacques Derrida.

… we are touching upon the limits and the greatest audacities of discourse in Western thought.

JAQUES DERRIDA,
WRITING AND DIFFÉRANCE

teachings, philosophy is a human, literary discourse like any other and cannot deal in timeless, abstract truths. He is famous for terms such as '*différance*' and 'deconstruction'. He lectures in the USA and is currently Director of Studies at the École des Haute Etudes en Science Sociales. He is a prolific writer, but his works are specialized, experimental and playful, and are difficult for the uninitiated. Some key texts are *Of Grammatology*, *Writing and Différance* and *Spectres of Marx*. His interests range across literature, philosophy, the arts, ethics, religion and politics.

Michel Foucault (1926–84)

French thinker Foucault developed a suspicion of power behind all knowledge – who tells you what is true? He followed Nietzsche in seeking to trace the foundations of an opinion or dogma, the 'archaeology' of a discipline. He wrote widely on a number of cross-cultural issues, such as how we have treated madness, crime and punishment, and sexuality. Key texts are *Madness and Civilization*, *The History of Sexuality* and *Archaeology of Knowledge*.

Luce Irigaray (1932–)

A French feminist thinker and practising analyst, Irigaray questions the masculine bias of much Western philosophy and seeks to rethink it. Her work is often playful, poetic and lyrical, rather than logical and systematic. Key texts are *Speculum of the Other Woman*, *This Sex Which is Not One* and *An Ethics of Sexual Difference*.

A discourse may poison, surround, encircle, imprison or liberate, heal, nourish, fertilize…

LUCE IRIGARAY,
JE, TU, NOUS – TOWARD A CULTURE OF DIFFERENCE

Julia Kristeva (1941–)

Kristeva is a Bulgarian-born feminist thinker who arrived to work in Paris in the 1960s. She worked with Derrida and other radical thinkers in the *Tel Quel* group, looking at literature and creativity, and then worked in the fields of sexuality, feminism, ethics and mental health. She has written a number of texts, which

Postfeminist writer and psychoanalyst Julia Kristeva.

include *Tales of Love*, *Strangers to Ourselves*, *New Maladies of the Soul* and *Black Sun: Depression and Melancholia*. She is Professor of Linguistics at the University of Paris VII, and a psychoanalyst.

Jacques Lacan (1901–81)

Lacan developed the work of Freud in France, influenced by the surrealists. His distinctive idea was that our 'souls' or selves are formed by language as we grow. There is no actual 'self' within us. Language – the

Psychotherapist
Jacques Lacan.

> *But I think that responsibility for the other man, or, if you like, the epiphany of the human face, constitutes a penetration of the crust, so to speak, of 'being preserving in its being' and preoccupied with itself.*
>
> EMMANUEL LEVINAS,
> *VIOLENCE OF THE FACE*

world of human discourse — helps us to form an identity. Lacan's work has influenced a number of postmodern thinkers, especially Irigaray and Kristeva.

Emmanuel Levinas (1906–95)

Levinas came to France in the 1930s from Lithuania. He was of Jewish background, and found the preoccupation with being and self-identity too one-sided in Western philosophy, introducing the concept of the other — any other sentient being, animal, human or God; we are primarily relational beings. Levinas brought ethics into the study of existence. His

Philosopher
Emmanuel
Levinas.

key texts are *Time and the Other*, *Totality and Infinity* and *Otherwise Than Being*.

Jean-François Lyotard (1925–99)

Lyotard taught at the University of Paris VIII at Vincennes, and at the University of California at Irvine. He abandoned the classical attempt of Western philosophy to form total explanations and eternal truths. He rejected grand narratives, which try to tie up the whole of reality, as impossible. We, as human beings, can only have partial insights. His key text is *The Postmodern Condition*.

The French Connection

There is an indisputable Gallic connection with the rise of postmodernism. There are various reasons why this is so.

You may have noticed the preponderance of French men and women in the previous lists. Why so? The Continental schools of philosophy have taken a different turn from the Anglo-Saxon ones, which remain more analytical and logical. Perhaps this says something about France, with its social dynamic of the intellectual outsider over

It may, of course, be that... treating French 'philosophy' as the same sort of enterprise as 'philosophy' in the English-speaking world only distorts our understanding of it — like treating French boules as the same game as English bowls...

ERIC MATTHEWS,
*TWENTIETH-CENTURY
FRENCH PHILOSOPHY*

against the strict codification of laws and the deeply ingrained social norms. The culture of the street café and the Left Bank in Paris has gossiped and debated postmodernism. Perhaps, too, the deeply Catholic roots of that land have shaped things. There is an openness to the mystical and the eternal, and to questions that skirt the edge of reason and reality.

These are guesses. Postmodernism is very much a Gallic phenomenon. Not only are some of the thinkers from a Catholic background, several are Jews. Some are from abroad, or have come as students or refugees from the East in their youth.

THE EVENTS OF 1968

May 1968 saw student riots in the Nanterre region of Paris. The students were joined by nearly 9 million workers and many intellectuals, such as the philosopher Jean-Paul Sartre (1905–80). They demanded better study conditions and better pay. The same year saw protests in London and the USA. This was a sign of a major shift in society and an attack on the Establishment. In the USA, the focus was on the war in Vietnam.

There is a definite spiritual and outsider tradition deeply rooted in postmodernism.

Left Bank café culture discusses philosophical issues easily and without social embarrassment.

Summing up

Postmodernism shares a number of basic tenets:

■ Human knowledge is limited to human discourse; we cannot have direct access to reality 'out there'.

■ Thus, grand narratives of any type, whether religious, philosophical or scientific, are limited and historically conditioned. They are flawed and incomplete by necessity. These narratives simply claim too much for themselves. There are only more local and partial narratives and insights possible.

■ Our generation is more ironically self-aware than any previous one. We realize that we are children of our time, and we play with ideas and styles from other eras quite deliberately.

■ There are competing truth claims, types of discourse, forms of knowledge and lifestyles. Tolerance, openness and flexibility are the order of the day.

There is a suspicion of any undergirding foundation for truth that justifies our positions. We see things how we see them and impose a certain degree of order and meaning upon the world. But what does that reduce us to? What happens to the 'self', human rights, God and faith, for example? These are just some of the issues that will be teased out in the rest of this book.

WHAT IS TRUTH?

Our senses perceive the world around us – but how real are those perceptions? The image we see is the result of the wonderful mechanisms of the eye. Electrical signals travel to the brain, which interprets what is 'seen'. The same is true for all the other senses – information from a physical stimulus is processed in the brain. Clearly these things must bear some resemblance to the truth or we would not have survived in this world as a species.

But how objective is our experience? Could our minds be playing tricks on us, to an extent? Are we seeing only what we want to see?

Solid road and colourful scenery. Can we doubt that this is real?

If a tree falls in a forest, miles from anyone, is there a sound? There is a disturbance of air and an impact, but there is only a sound as such if someone is there to hear it. Sound is, at least in part, a human construct, an interpretation of the brain.

There are many examples of the brain's power over the senses: LSD trips can seem frighteningly real; amputated limbs can still cause pain. It is very hard not to think that things are how we perceive them to be. Philosophers have often struggled with the idea of what is true, and of how we see the world: the idealists, empiricists and existentialists have all contributed to the discussion. This question goes straight to the heart of the postmodern condition.

Contents

Turn on, tune in, drop out.
TIMOTHY LEARY

Idealism

Idealism tried to solve the reality puzzle by an appeal
to thought, the mind and the thinking subject. To
approach postmodernism, we need to probe the roots
of idealism to see what is being reacted against.

The 17th-century idealists
saw reality as a product of
the mind, or of God's thought.
The French philosopher
René Descartes (1596–1650)
emerged as the first modern
philosopher by casting doubt
upon everything: maybe his
mind was playing tricks, or a
devil was deceiving him. What
data could he trust as true? He
could only find a secure point
in his own thoughts: *'Cogito, ergo
sum'* – 'I think, therefore I am.'

Descartes laid the
foundations for the modern

Mathematician
and philosopher
René Descartes.
Portrait by
Frans Hals
(1580–1666).

scientific method of observation and testing, but in his opinion the surest, true, fixed point in life was the inner mind: the consciousness. This division of mind/body, or the spiritual/physical, is known as 'Cartesian dualism' from the Latin for Descartes – Cartesius.

To be or not to be?

The English philosopher and churchman George Berkeley (1685–1753) took this further. He argued that the only reason an object existed, say a chair, was because we thought it into being. If we left the room, it might vanish, except for the presence and power of God's mind that gave it continued existence. This made the mental and the abstract the most real thing in life, with the eternal verities of mathematics being of more substance than the fleeting beauty of a snowflake, so subtle, unique and intricately designed. Mathematics gave general, universal principles that were calculable and predictable.

Philosopher and churchman George Berkeley.

There is a vast difference between the mind and the body, in that the body by its very nature is always divisible, while the mind is completely indivisible. For when I consider the mind, or rather when I consider myself simply as a thinking thing, I find I can distinguish no parts within myself, and I clearly discern that I am a thing utterly one and complete.

RENÉ DESCARTES,
MEDITATIONS

Although Descartes is known as a French philosopher, he wrote most of his major works in Holland, where he settled in 1629.

Empiricism

The empiricists sought to trust only what could be discerned through the five senses, only that which could be measured and observed.

Descartes had primarily sought a fixed, immutable point of truth within the mental/spiritual realm, but he also pioneered the scientific method of observation: proposing a hypothesis, testing the data and revising the hypothesis accordingly. The Englishman John Locke (1632–1704) championed the empirical cause, veering away from the idealist position. Locke sought truth in rational analysis of exterior data. We interact with the world around us, a very real, given environment. Our perceptions are generated by this interaction with our sensory experience. He shunned any idea of innate wisdom and immortal souls. The newborn child was a tabula rasa, a conceptual blank slate, waiting to form knowledge and perceptions from interaction with life.

Empiricists sought different fixed points from the idealists. Their fixed points originated in the reality of the physical world and its natural laws (such as gravity), which had to be assumed for the scientific method to work.

Kant's spectacles

The German thinker Immanuel Kant (1724–1804) sought a

BLACK SWANS

Some thinkers saw limitations in the empirical world view. The English philosopher David Hume (1711–76) was a radical sceptic who thought that human reason was incapable of comprehending reality in total. We might sift through data and experiment, but we might not be aware of a vital piece of information that would change our view of things. Thus, for example, he famously argued that if we only ever saw white swans, then we would logically deduce that there were only white swans. But what if one day we met a black swan? In fact, when Dutch explorer Willem de Vlamingh reported that he had seen black swans in Australia in 1697, most Europeans did not believe him, as they thought that all swans were white.

Kant was such a creature of habit that people set their watches by the time he took a walk each day. He only once neglected to take this regular exercise, as he was so absorbed in a book: Jean-Jacques Rousseau's *Émile*.

Philosopher Immanuel Kant.

Two things fill the heart with ever renewed and increasing awe and reverence, the more often and the more steadily we meditate upon them: the starry firmament above and the moral law within.

IMMANUEL KANT,
CRITIQUE OF PURE REASON

middle way between empiricism and idealism. He coined the terms 'noumena' and 'phenomena'. The noumena was the world of reality as it is, in itself. The phenomena was the world of appearances and sense perceptions – our angle on reality. The one did not totally refer to the other. Perception involved a dialectic between what actually is 'out there' and how we see things.

We filter reality through the spectacles of our sense perception. There is no possibility of stepping outside this. Only God can do that. Kant appealed to God's existence as the one foundational point that was sure. God gave form and order to a world that we could not directly know, and our minds formed pictures, models and conceptual constructs. In other words, if God is, then truth is out there.

Kant's middle way had a far-reaching influence upon postmodernism. The seeds of this later system of thought can be found here.

We sift reality through the lenses of our sense perception.

Existentialism

Existentialist philosophy failed to solve the reality puzzle. Despite its rejection of external absolutes, it depended upon the self in an almost Cartesian sense. Postmodernism was to question the fact of the 'self'.

The early part of the 20th century saw a revival of the fortunes of idealism in a new guise. Various thinkers asserted the givenness of mind or consciousness as primary for our knowledge of the world.

The German philosopher Edmund Husserl (1859–1938) said that the only sure point was in our experience of consciousness. He sought to reduce thought and speculation to pure experience by a series of reductions, stripping away distracting ideas and theories. We are only present to ourselves. This is the immediacy of experience, the only unshakeable content. He defined phenomenology – the study of existence and the things that happen (phenomena) – as the experience of things in our consciousness only.

Being

Husserl's student, Martin Heidegger (1889–1976), followed on with talk of 'being'. According to Heidegger, before our conscious experience, we were in the world as a given. *Dasein* ('being there') means that we are thrown into the world, as clay is thrown onto a potter's wheel. It also involves moral choices and we can live (be) in an authentic or inauthentic manner, as a free agent or as pushed, pulled and controlled by the many.

Existence precedes essence.

JEAN-PAUL SARTRE, *BEING AND NOTHINGNESS*

Jean-Paul Sartre

Heidegger's form of phenomenology, or the study of being, led on to existentialist philosophy as propounded by Jean-Paul Sartre (1905–80): the inner life, experience, consciousness, mind was supreme. Sartre compared the mind with non-conscious objects, such as a paper knife, which were predetermined in their design. We were free.

Consciousness was primary,

but he refused to believe in a fixed, static self. What we are is what we become. Life flows. A person is a lifetime's project. The freedom to choose to be is a frightening prospect.

This philosophy can be caricatured as 'do your own

the consciousness. Kantian philosophy rejected this belief, and, later, postmodernism would overturn it. Nothing, not even knowledge or existence itself, can be really present, say the postmodernists. All is filtered, all is interpreted — we cannot

We find ourselves thrown into existence, like clay on a wheel. This experience is prior to any form of self-consciousness.

thing', a distorted form of which inspired the hedonism and libertinism of the 1960s, but Sartre and his followers had a far greater sense of responsibility and belief in quality of life: for them, experience and existence really were present to us, directly in

step outside our sense perceptions and our human language. There are no absolute vantage points, outside or within.

Are There Any 'Hard Facts'?

What truth is science based upon? How much relies on the imaginative, creative faculty rather than neutral observation?

Empiricism has left its legacy with scientific materialism, the belief that the physical world is given and primary. What we can see and touch and measure is really real. The popular understanding of science is that it gives us sure knowledge of the world around us, hard facts rather than theories. Upon closer examination, this picture might be rather exaggerated.

The scientific method works by repeated observation.

THE UNCERTAINTY PRINCIPLE

The German scientist Werner Karl Heisenberg (1901–76) formulated his famous uncertainty principle in 1926. This stated that the more precisely you measure the position of a particle, the less accurately you can determine its momentum. We cannot accurately measure the two simultaneously; we cannot grasp the total picture.

A theory of why something happens will be devised, and tests conducted to confirm or deny this. The results might make researchers think again. Sometimes, we might have to rethink and rethink, retest and retest until we emerge with a theory that fits the result. It is not always cut and dried.

Pulsars are stellar objects that emit regular bursts of radio waves. One such lies in the direction of the Carina Nebula, shown here. We can only determine what is happening by a series of guesses and ideas.

Think, for example, of the discovery of pulsars. Two researchers, Jocelyn Bell and Anthony Hewish, discovered objects in the heavens that were emitting regular pulses of radio waves. Their first

Mind bending?

A further difficulty is that some observations contradict previously accepted ways of thinking. Light behaves in some situations as waves and in others as particles. It is not

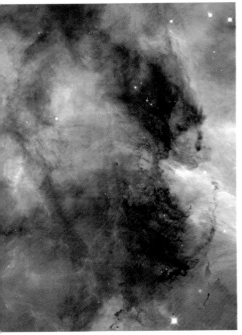

The uncertainty principle had profound implications for the way in which we view the world. Even after fifty years, they have not been fully appreciated by many philosophers, and are still the subject of much controversy.

STEPHEN HAWKING,
A BRIEF HISTORY OF TIME

thought was that these were alien messages. They called the four pulsars LGM1–4 in their early research, standing for 'Little Green Man'. They moved through a few more theories before settling on the most likely explanation: stars that emit radio waves, now known as pulsars.

an either/or situation, but a both/and! It used to be thought that waves and particles were completely separate. This flies in the face of the conventional laws of logic, which state (following from Aristotle) that there cannot be an inherent contradiction. Hence, modern science struggles with a supra-rational concept; reality is bigger than our definitions. Hard facts thus give way to models, ideas and constructs that are the best way we have of understanding a subject at the moment.

Subject/Object

Quantum physics has turned thinking inside out and has allowed us to recognize the role of subjectivity in experiments.

Heisenberg helped to define quantum mechanics, which rethought the structure of the physical universe. One feature of this was the blurring of the edges between subject and object, or observer and observed. Everything is linked and part of the whole. Our very presence, as well as our senses and cognitive limitations, affects the experiments and the results. We see only in part. Reality cannot be totally measured, and deterministic philosophies of science – where everything can be precisely predicted – are now in tatters.

Quantum mechanics has introduced an element of

The world view and sense perceptions of the researcher affect the results of the test. Charles Herbert Best (right), the Canadian physiologist who assisted in the discovery of insulin, in the laboratory with his assistant.

random unpredictability, and even the old laws of physics, such as gravity, are seen as observations of what *usually* happens, rather than fixed, objective laws. Remember Hume and his black swans: what aspects of the universe have we not observed? Maybe things happen that we cannot currently detect.

The will to power

Nietzsche wrote about the slippery value of 'truth'. Whose truth was it? It all depended upon where you were standing.

So what is truth? A mobile army of metaphors, metonyms, anthropomorphisms — in short, an aggregate of human relationships which, poetically and rhetorically heightened, become transposed and elaborated, and which, after protracted popular usage, pose as fixed, canonical, obligatory. Truths are illusions whose illusionness is overlooked.

FRIEDRICH NIETZSCHE,
*ON TRUTH AND FALSEHOOD
IN AN EXTRA-MORAL SENSE*

APES

An example of how we can influence test results can be seen in studies of apes in the latter half of the 20th century. In 1950s USA, chimpanzees were housed in rectangular cages in rows and their interactions were observed. They were being organized like human middle-class suburbia without anyone realizing it, and their actions were set against these traits and values.

Postfeminist awareness watched the apes in the wild, closer to nature, but agendas were still to the fore; ideas about male/female roles, along with hunting and child-rearing, coloured what was seen. Ideologies had been imposed upon data.

Power was the key; facts were sifted and twisted for propaganda purposes. He spoke of the fundamental, human 'will to power', a striving to dominate and control that individuals and groups manifest. Nietzsche also pointed out (before Freud and psychoanalysis) that we are not just rational beings, but passionate beings, with hidden drives and desires that form our ideas and view of the world. These drives took in 'the most questionable elements in life… the awareness that creation and destruction are inseparable'.

Archaeology of 'Truth'

Who decides what is true? Truths often have a history of interpretation, and philosophers have uncovered their 'archaeology', the ideological strata showing their development.

Science, for Nietzsche, was an imposter, pretending to fixed, neutral, objective knowledge when such a thing was impossible. Scientific explanations are not really explanations; they merely produce more and more complex descriptions. Fire burning becomes chemical reaction, but it is still, in essence, as magical as it was to those who first harnessed its power. Nietzsche rejected the worship of knowledge for knowledge's sake, and wanted to establish its underlying use. If such knowledge threatened life, then it was an error (think of pollution and nuclear bombs). He remarked, prophetically, 'The fact that science as we practise it today is possible proves that the elementary instincts which protect life have ceased to function.' Nietzsche probed further, suggesting that values and concepts all had a history – in his terms a 'genealogy' – and were not hard, objective truths.

Foucault's 'archaeology'

The French philosopher Michel Foucault (1926–84) followed on from Nietzsche, arguing that all knowledge was influenced by power play. Foucault is usually classed as 'postmodern' – and some even claim Nietzsche as an early prophet of the movement.

Foucault wrote about the sociology of knowledge, focusing on attitudes to sex, madness and the treatment of criminals. He spoke of 'archaeologies' in a discipline. These were strata, or layers, of influences, eras that defined the ideas of their time. His research did involve detailed historical study, unearthing old

Philosopher Michel Foucault.

Atomic explosion. How 'true' is the knowledge that allowed this to be?

THE ARCHAEOLOGY OF MORALS

Nietzsche delved into the genealogy of morality with a vengeance. He studied early societies in which the nobles were the virtuous and the low-born were weak and contemptible. This 'high-born, low-born' value system was the aristocratic layer in the archaeology of morals. The priestly layer came from an obsession with ritual purity and the subsequent virtue of suppressing and denying parts of our human nature. He concluded that morals had a varying history, relative to different ages, and were founded upon far more than merely altruistic actions.

books and texts, but Foucault used this term in its wider sense of reaching down and seeking to explain why a set of ideas had come to be. This was not because 'truth' had been discovered, but people had ideas that came from social mores; power systems guarded these until challenged by paradigm shifts.

Foucault noted that science was not the neutral discipline it claimed to be. There were rivalries and competing theories. How hard was it for some researchers to have their ideas listened to because these went against the system? How accurate could observation be when the preconceptions of the observer could not help but come into play? What might a medieval person make of an event compared with someone from our century, and someone from a thousand years in the future? What was missed out and passed over because it did not fit?

What is Real Any More?

The hyper-real theories of French postmodern thinker Jean Baudrillard (1929–) engage with the mass media and the manipulation of truth.

In an age of mass media and fast, international communications, warfare has entered a new era. Baudrillard is not just talking about smart bombs and laser-targeted attacks, but the instant replay of footage, analysed, dissected and spun by the politicians and the media. Modern wars are cyber wars, and Baudrillard raises questions about media hype and manipulation. Are we really seeing what is happening? Who says? Selective presentation and editing can change what we see and believe.

Baudrillard famously stated that the Gulf War did not happen (at least not in the old, conventional sense of a war). It was a TV-screen drama. The facts were selected and interpreted by both sides. Saddam Hussein had his rent-a-crowds and the USA spun their propaganda while maintaining their interests, keeping Saddam in power, but having him crush the Shi'ites and Kurdish opposition. Stability then reigned. Baudrillard quipped that it was like 'safe sex', making war with a condom on!

He aroused more controversy with his work on American society – it is, on the one hand, a utopia where people are outrageously wealthy, but at the same time it is rife with social disintegration. He caused offence and complained that people had no sense of irony.

> *… any order exists only to be disobeyed, attacked, exceeded and dismantled.*
>
> JEAN BAUDRILLARD, *FATAL STRATEGIES*

Seduction techniques

Baudrillard developed a strategy of seduction – a subversive gesture, statement or posture that refused to play the usual social game of power relationships. By this, neither party can be an oppressor or reduced to the level of an object to be controlled – compare the flirtation of a couple, moving closer to each other, testing and teasing. Baudrillard felt that we could

The real Bogart is dead and gone, but his hyper-real image flickers on. Still from *Casablanca* (1942) showing, from left to right, Louis (Satchmo) Armstrong, Humphrey Bogart and Ingrid Bergman.

HYPER-REALITY

Baudrillard feels that reality is dead, and we live in a vast Disneyland of hyper-reality. Hyper-reality is a state in which signs have a life of their own – disconnected from reality, and free-floating. The sign was once a reflection of the real, but now it is part of an elaborate game, played for its own sake. The real might be absent or gone, but the sign lives on. Humphrey Bogart is dead, but he flickers on a thousand screens all over the world in reruns of *Casablanca*, looking at Ingrid Bergman and saying, 'Here's looking at you, kid!'

subvert power structures and thus clear the decks to think more clearly, but he was sceptical about being able to achieve any real or lasting social change. Reality is dead…?

Postmodernism has questioned that 'truth' simply exists, and it is suspicious and cynical about who tells us what. This extends into our use of language, which is the topic of the next chapter.

Summing up

Truth is a loaded term; social norms and power structures try to define what is 'true'. Ideas can often have a history, and ideological archaeology digs deep to uncover it. The 'will to power' reveals that people want to control and manipulate thought and belief. Even science does not always deal in hard facts, but theories and guesses, models that sometimes defy reason or go beyond it.

DECONSTRUCTION

Ferdinand de Saussure (1857–1913), a Swiss professor of linguistics, revolutionized the study of language. He saw language as a system of signs – not timeless, abstract ideas, but socially and culturally constructed signs. He differentiated between language and words. Language was the whole system with underlying structures and rules. These structures were universal.

Saussure defined a sign as a combination of an object and a name or sound for it. The object was the signified and the name was the signifier. Signified + signifier = the sign. For example, the word 'cow' is a signifier for the animal, which is the signified.

The primitive totem pole is not just about ancient mythology, but depicts social hierarchy and world view. Lévi-Strauss held that the primitive mind was not outside nature, but very much a self-conscious part of it.

Together, this word and the image of the creature make up the sign for it.

Saussure argued that the representation of an object by a name/sound was quite arbitrary. The individual signifiers were different across cultures, but the underlying rules were constant. They turned on the principle of binary opposition, a system of opposites, which contrast and compare. So, signified/signifier stand in a row with concepts such as light/dark, black/white, true/false and so on.

The French anthropologist Claude Lévi-Strauss (1908–) developed this structuralist study of linguistics into a study of human society. The human world and nature were two opposites, and thinking or speaking occurs in the interaction between these two spheres. He sought underlying structures in symbols, customs and gestures across cultures. These were the deep structures behind words, stories and artefacts.

Barthes and Derrida used the foundations laid by Saussure and Lévi-Strauss to build their own theories.

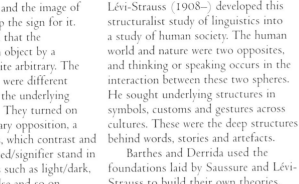

Contents

The anthropologist respects history, but he does not accord it a special value… He conceives it as a study complementary to his own; one of them unfurls the range of human societies in time, the other in space.

CLAUDE LÉVI-STRAUSS,
THE SAVAGE MIND

Deep Structures and Scepticism

Roland Barthes' literary studies declared 'the death of the author' by appealing to unconscious, deep structures that control stories and keep on resurfacing across the ages.

For structuralists, meaning tended to be located in the deep, underlying structures and not in the more superficial, conscious thoughts of the writer. Literary critics sought unconscious layers in works of fiction, seeing these as more important and revealing than the conscious. Private, personal and intuitive meanings were left aside.

An example of this approach is in Barthes' analysis of the works of the French

TOTEM AND TABOO

Sigmund Freud speculated that one root of universal human guilt lay in a primeval murder: sons ganged up on the tribal father and killed him to share his power and his access to the tribe's women. This theory fired Freud's views of religion: the idea of 'sin' stemmed from the murder; God as Father was an idealized, internalized father figure needed when the real one was murdered.

We can, through art, be intensely moved by something that does not exist, never has existed, and never could exist.

ROLAND BARTHES

playwright Jean Racine (1639–99). Barthes argued that Racine did not really know what he was doing when he was writing. Racine's tragedies, whatever their storyline, were really about power and jealousy. One person has power over another but is unable to find love. Barthes thought that this reflected the eternal conflict between fathers and sons used by Freud in *Totem and Taboo*.

Structuralist interpretations can be given to many works of art and literature. Recent studies of John's Gospel, for example, have displayed the following underlying, deep structure: a quest, a sender, a receiver of the mission, a helper, an opponent. Thus, God sends Jesus to redeem the world, helped by the Holy Spirit, and he is opposed by

Satan, the Romans and Jewish leaders.

Barthes went so far as to speak of 'the death of the author'. The author is turned into a mere *scripteur*, like the manuscript copiers of medieval monasteries. The writer has within 'neither passions, humours, feelings nor impressions. Only this immense dictionary from which he takes a writing activity which can never cease.'

Surely, Barthes went too far? Authors do respond to and display underground drives and structures in language, culture and the psyche, but they are also people in their own right, making certain conscious choices. They may even knowingly use primal themes and imagery.

On 26 March 1980, Barthes was knocked down by a laundry van in a Parisian street and killed. This was just after having lunch with Michel Foucault and François Mitterand, just before the latter was elected President of France.

49

Free-Floating

Roland Barthes studied popular culture using the concept of free-floating signifiers to analyse its conventions. Social convention, in Barthes' view, determined meaning.

Barthes went further than traditional structuralists. He focused on Saussure's point about the arbitrary nature of signs and pushed this to its limits. Signifiers were free-floating, in a stream of words. Who decides what signifies what? This aligned him with the position of post-structuralism and postmodernism.

Traffic lights could, in theory, have used any colours for Stop/Caution/Go. Each nation might have had a different system. True, a form of social contract might have harmonized them as communications improved, but they were free-floating in their meaning – in their essence.

Wrestling and fashion

Barthes applied structural analysis to mass, popular culture. He famously observed wrestling matches and highlighted the codified structures and the art of the performance. Wrestling is not a genuine fight, and the audience are collaborators – they know

When the hero or the villain of the drama, the man who was seen a few minutes earlier possessed by moral rage, magnified into a sort of metaphysical sign, leaves the wrestling hall, impassive, anonymous, carrying a small suitcase and arm-in-arm with his wife, no one can doubt that wrestling holds that power of transmutation which is common to the Spectacle and to Religious Worship.

ROLAND BARTHES,
THE WORLD OF WRESTLING

Barthes wrote his series of observations on popular culture in monthly magazine pieces between 1954 and 1956, covering topics as diverse as Citroën cars, the face of Greta Garbo and jet pilots. These were collected and published as *Mythologies* in 1957.

it is all pretence. The matches have their own conventions, such as hitting the deck with the flat of the hand to signal submission. Barthes argued

Wrestling – savagery and natural aggression, or performance art?

that these conventions could be subverted and swapped with anything else. The loser could sing the national anthem, for example, to signify defeat. But

Fashions on the catwalk – who decides what is desirable?

or purity of the fabric, or the artisan skills of the designer or maker. Fashion was ruled by consumerism and big business. Consumer preferences were controlled by the industry, and peer pressure responded to what people said was 'in' that season.

A sea of signs

Baudrillard took Barthes' analysis further, seeing capitalist consumerism as a vast, semiotic sea of signs that drowns everything. The signs change rapidly, and in the process destroy traditional ways of life. 'Living' materials, such as wood and cotton and even sunlight, are replaced by synthetics – plastics, electric and neon lights and so on. It is only a short step to Baudrillard's world of hyper-reality, where the sign has a virtual existence of its own, free-floating in a new sense, cut off from its original roots.

society has agreed rules of signification. Humans live in society and not in raw nature.

Barthes also observed the fashion industry and saw conventions ruling there too. The value of certain garments did not depend upon the rarity

Logocentrism

Derrida has challenged any attempts to root and ground truth in anything external to language.

Saussure made a huge mistake in the eyes of post-structuralist thinkers. He assumed that you could write about and perceive language and all its mechanisms and rules from an external vantage point. According to the post-structuralists, we cannot. We live in language. This is what is meant by Barthes' statement that everything is contained in language. When he wrote about fashion in *Système de la mode* in 1967, he said in an interview, 'fashion exists only through the discourse on it'.

Foundationalism

Saussure's semiotics are seen as yet another attempt at foundationalism, the quest to find secure and fixed points of truth external to our subjective experience.

The Greeks had often seen reason as the guiding light of truth, and Plato (427–347 BCE) had the world of unseen ideals. These were the master forms and shapes of everything that exists, the ideal form of a chair, the ideal man, the ideal sun. These abstractions were eternal,

Can we find a sure foundation for thought and understanding? Victoria Falls, Zimbabwe.

unlike the changing, imperfect forms on earth.

Medieval philosophy held that God and his revelation were such foundational truths. The Enlightenment tried various tacks – the French philosopher René Descartes had the existence of the *cogito* ('I think') and the regularities of mathematics; the empiricists had that which could be measured. Husserl and the later existentialists tried experience itself.

[Undecidability is] a truth we must refuse to believe.

JACQUES DERRIDA

For postmodernists, everything is filtered through our language and our interpretation. Kant's spectacles are upon our noses. If – and that is a big 'if' for some thinkers – there is an external truth, then we are not able to perceive it as human beings.

that abstract, philosophical points are tied to particular words. For Derrida, meanings are stabilized by the society of the time and not by any external fixed point: 'there is nothing outside the text'.

Here, he is very much a post-structuralist, building upon the free-floating signifiers of Barthes. He develops this further in a programme of reading texts that sees beyond the narrow confines of binary opposites. He coined the term 'undecidability'.

Logocentrism

Jacques Derrida rails against logocentrism – the idea that words have fixed meanings, and

Derrida was proposed for an honorary degree at the University of Cambridge in 1992. This is usually a formality, but four dons refused to support him. Eventually, he was awarded the degree in a ballot of 336 votes to 204. Most of those proposing him were from the English Faculty, but Derrida was a philosopher, though one who writes of philosophy as a literary tradition.

UNDECIDABILITY

Sometimes we meet indeterminate categories that are neither/nor. The zombie and the android in science fiction stand in this role. In real life, who decides who are the enemy and the ally, or the stranger and the friend? What role do the media and government have in trying to control our thoughts in this area? So, in the First World War, the troops kicked footballs and swapped photos on that first wartime Christmas in 1914. The soldiers remembered that they were human, first and foremost, and the war machine and its us/them uniforms were forgotten, mercifully, if only for a short time. Or, in Jesus' parable of the Good Samaritan, a 'bad guy', a disrespected foreigner, becomes the hero. Life just isn't always so simple that we can say 'Yes/No' to everything.

Writing: Cure or Poison?

Derrida's attempt to subvert Western philosophy resides in the debate about the value of speech over writing.

Derrida sees writing itself as an example of something that is undecidable. He studies Socrates' defence of the value of speech over writing in Plato's *Phaedrus*. Socrates never actually wrote anything himself, and he argued that writing dulls the memory and stops people thinking for themselves. It is a lifeless, external thing, like a portrait painting of someone. In dialogue, you can watch your opponent, interject, question and turn the discussion in new ways. A written piece is fixed. In ancient myths, writing is a *pharmakon* for memory and wisdom – a 'cure' or 'remedy'. However, it can also mean 'poison'.

In *Phaedrus*, Socrates retells the myth of the Egyptian god Theuth. He was an inventor, and writing was one of his ideas. He presented all of his inventions to the king, Thamus. Thamus listened, but questioned the wisdom of writing. He declared that it was a *pharmakon* in the negative sense of poison, for it would do all that Socrates had argued. It would make people lazy and

THE MOVIES

Reading a film script is a poor substitute for seeing the film. The dialogue is meant to be enacted, 'lived', 'enfleshed'. Derrida does not deny that living speech can be dynamic and more rewarding than mere reading, but writing has its value, and can be involved in the dynamic too. Interestingly, Derrida is a great fan of the cinema: '*c'est sorte de fascination hypnotique*' ('it has a kind of hypnotic fascination'). He speaks of '*la fantomalité*' ('phantomlikeness') or '*la spectralité*' ('of spectres', 'spectrality') of the cinema, where we relate to images that are neither alive nor dead (undecidable), that have a communal effect upon the audience and tease out our emotions. In an interview in *Cahiers du cinéma*, he made the following comment: '*C'est la signe d'un "penser ensemble" qui me semble primordial.*' ('It is the sign of a "thinking together" that seems to me to be primordial.')

stop them memorizing. It would freeze ideas and not allow them to be debated in living disputation. It would externalize what should be internal.

Derrida plays with this dual role of *pharmakon* (cure/poison) as undecidability. He sees Socrates' argument as based upon binary oppositions, where one concept is always preferred to the other. If we take the following statement, 'Speech is better than writing, because it is internal to the mind or memory, involves living people and engages with the essence of wisdom rather than its written appearance,' then we have:

◆ speech/writing
◆ good/bad
◆ internal/external
◆ living/non-living
◆ essence/appearance.

Derrida notes that, in the Egyptian myth, the king returned the *pharmakon* to its inventor as decided. Much of classical philosophy has treated writing in this way, and Derrida wants to subvert this tradition and return its undecidability. The truth is that we cannot draw such a clear distinction between speech and writing. Writing can spur one to thought, start discussions, and present the essence of ideas to new generations. It cannot be confined to internal/external. It is a 'beyond' category: working beyond the logic of binary opposition.

Texts are enclosed within the rules of human language, whether spoken or written: a text is a discourse and a discourse is a text.

Egyptian hieroglyphs from the temple of Luxor, Egypt.

Différance

Derrida coined a new term, '*différance*', to emphasize the role of writing and the value of spaces between words that moves beyond binary opposition.

Derrida picks up on the free-floating nature of signs. The arbitrary nature of their links with objects leads to a sense of cognitive slippage – thoughts and meanings move about, floating between different possibilities. They are not fixed, but variable and movable; meaning can slip too, as you read a text. Words can be given different interpretations and a text can be read in a new way. This slippage can be referred to as *aporia*, from the Greek word meaning 'no passage': moments of difficulty and doubt when reading a text that make you stop and rethink.

Rather than always having a fixed, rigid meaning, the actual meaning is deferred. Derrida is concerned to open texts to new readings rather than the dominant, Western ones. His term '*différance*' designates this slippage and openness – the difference between things, the deferment of meaning, the space between marks on a page that frames and defines them, the actual space between people talking.

Différance suggests 'to defer', 'to give space to'. It is the space that allows things to be, the negative spaces in a painting that allow the forms

How can an object with no utility, comprised predominantly of empty space, be such a meaningful sign?

THE 'EMPTY' EIFFEL TOWER

Barthes followed a similar line of reasoning to Derrida when he argued that some signs were more powerful, universal and suggestive because they were empty. Hence, the Eiffel Tower is 'this pure – virtually empty – sign that means everything'. He could say 'its form is empty but present, its meaning absent but full'.

This Zen-like use of paradox and space has profound consequences, not just for literary criticism but for attitudes to ethics and metaphysics. It reminds us that we are part of a scene, framed by life, and we have to relate to other things and people around us. We are not isolated souls, as with Descartes, or confined in the solipsism, the closed-in, self-absorption of existentialism. Our logic cannot be the whole truth; we cannot capture reality in concepts. The subversive spaces open things up.

> *… deconstruction… insisted not on multiplicity for itself but on the heterogeneity, the difference, the disassociation, which is absolutely necessary for the relation to the other.*
>
> JACQUES DERRIDA,
> ROUNDTABLE DISCUSSION AT
> VILLANOVA UNIVERSITY IN 1994

of people and chairs to appear, the hole that allows a wheel to be. It is nothing, but nothing allows something to be. He had to create a new word – *'différance'* – for no word existed to fit this definition. Derrida is playful in his writing, and sometimes writes *'différance* is…' with a line crossed through it.

Derrida's rejection of fixed points and foundational truths subverts the simplistic vision of Western metaphysics that works from an origin to a stream of causes and accidents. Life is too diffuse and elusive for that. He refuses easy answers, but does not claim that anyone can ever truly do away with metaphysics, for the 'big questions' always remain with us: questions of ultimate concern.

Deconstruction is…

Deconstruction is not a defined method or a systematic programme, but a way of reading a text that shows its influences and its slippages – little details passed over or missed out that suggest other views and possible interpretations.

Derrida does not seek to formulate a precise programme of methodology to criticize texts or to help us think more clearly and honestly. He does have a strategy, though, which he has compared to a virus, whether biological or computer. The virus has two effects – it derails normal routes of communication and it opens up meaning by finding concepts that are undecidable. This strategy he has sometimes called 'deconstruction'.

Deconstruction is often misconstrued as sceptical and destructive, like tearing down an edifice for the sheer fun of it. Derrida toyed with the little-used French verb *déconstruire*, meaning 'to disassemble a

> *Deconstruction is not a method or some tool that you apply to something from the outside. Deconstruction is something which happens and which happens inside…*
> JACQUES DERRIDA

machine' (with the corollary that it can be reassembled). The noun 'deconstruction' is used for rearranging the grammar of words. Hence, for Derrida, deconstruction is positive. It shakes, subverts, dismays, but it only pulls apart to allow new things to be built, new meanings to be reached. It is a remedy for closed thinking.

Is/is not

Typically, Derrida playfully refuses to define deconstruction. When you say what it is, you have left out something else. Is it, indeed, a something that can be defined? The nearest he gets is to teach that it is fundamentally a suspicion of ever asking the question 'what is the essence of…?' because we can never get to a single, pure essence in any discourse. Analysis involves breaking things down into single units, and life doesn't allow this sort of treatment; critique makes you master of the subject and places you outside the text. But there is no outside, and you should always be learning, always open. His work preys upon existing texts, not seeking to pontificate, but to tease open, to caress and suggest. He inhabits the discourses he studies.

DECONSTRUCTING IDEOLOGIES

Though Derrida has used deconstruction for literary study, it can also be applied to movements and ideologies, to the 'text' of their

discourse, as it were. Just as a text can reveal slippages and open up new interpretations, and just as it can reveal various (perhaps subconscious) influences that the reader can discern, so too can the discourse used by any ideological group. What are their motives and hidden agendas? How have they put a certain spin on their teachings? What is their history? What power struggles have defined where they stand? Derrida claimed that his tactic of deconstruction was born out of his frustration as a young man with the ideology of the cold war, with the ideological impasse of the USA and the USSR both claiming the truth – a huge binary opposition in the political realm.

Binary opposition in action. Above, a naval trumpeter salutes the American flag, while, right, rockets are paraded in front of Soviet leaders in Red Square, Moscow.

Joker in the Pack

Derrida's playfulness casts him as a jester who challenges the court of received truth. His idea of the supplement opens up new meaning in a text.

Derrida's use of *différance* and deconstruction acts as a subversive influence in the history of philosophy. For one thing, philosophy is studied as literature, and is analysed with all the tools and critical insights appropriate to literary studies. Philosophy has been primarily a written text, and yet, amazingly, speech has been privileged over writing from Socrates onwards. Derrida's methods show up this dichotomy for all to see. His tactics are thus akin to those of a medieval jester who dared speak out against the monarch using wit and wordplay.

Deconstructing Lévi-Strauss

Derrida deconstructed the work of Lévi-Strauss in *Of Grammatology*. He studied the section entitled 'A Writing Lesson' (see box) and showed how it presupposed a general theory of writing rather than an established one. He points out that this was not a real introduction of writing to the

A WRITING LESSON

The anthropologist Claude Lévi-Strauss presented a theory of writing in an incident he recorded in *Tristes tropiques*, published in 1955. This acts as an autobiography, chronicling his initiation into social anthropology. The section called 'A Writing Lesson' is about the Nambikwara, a Latin American tribe who have no writing system. After staying among them for a while, Lévi-Strauss notices that some of them are producing horizontal lines on paper, which, he assumes, is a meaningless imitation of him writing up his notes. The chief seems to show more of an insight into the function of writing,

and he copies the same horizontal lines down after speaking with Lévi-Strauss, definitely copying him. He pretends that these lines mean something and 'reads' them out.

Later, when visiting other tribes, they are suspicious of the presence of a foreigner, and so the chief proceeds with the customary exchange of gifts to placate them. He pretends to read out a list of gifts from his pad, a recital that lasts for two hours. Lévi-Strauss reflects how the symbol or form of writing has been taken without any understanding, but has been used to enhance social prestige.

Nambikwara, but only an imitation, a ritual. It is an incursion, too rapid to be understood or integrated without the usual and necessary long years of apprenticeship. Derrida also shows that Lévi-Strauss is seeing the tribe in a wistful light; they are not natural innocents corrupted by Westerners, but have a history of violence of their own.

Supplement

Western philosophy has seen writing as a supplement to speech, meaning an adjunct, something that comes after, secondary. Derrida recasts the role and value of the supplement. He begins by noting that in the Egyptian myth that Plato uses (in a Hellenized version) of Thoth and Ammon, a father/son opposition is in play. Thoth is the son of Ammon. The son is supplement to the king, and will one day usurp and replace him. The supplement replaces and threatens: 'The king is dead. Long live the king!' But the king opposes himself in a sense. Son versus father = king versus king. There is something undecidable about all of this.

The moon can eclipse the sun; a son can usurp the king. A supplement is not necessarily an inferior.

Wrapping Up

The free play of signifiers has perhaps been exaggerated, and although we do need more poetic and imaginative forms of expression, we are limited by our bodies and senses. We do, after all, live in an actual world.

Post-structuralist thinkers have pointed out the rigidity and mechanistic nature of structuralist analysis. It is ultimately reductionist, reducing everything to certain patterns and formulas. It is logocentric in this sense, seeing reason, *logos*, as supreme.

The nature of arbitrary signifiers has shown up slippages in texts and thought systems. This has opened up meaning and our appreciation of reality. We can see much more about the nature of cultural influence, taboos, socialization and the ephemeral in the 'semiotic sea', the flow of words. Are things as fixed and structured as we once believed? Post-structuralists have found a place for the emotions and for the creative faculties in their view of reality and discourse.

Free play?

The post-structuralists, or the postmodernists, are often accused of abandoning meaning and seeing life as a vacuous, empty sea of signs, whereby the best we can do is to invent our own meanings. All becomes relative. Some veer close to this position, but others are more careful. Derrida does not want to deny that life has meaning; he just wants to open up the discourse as much as possible, look at things from all possible angles. A text does not offer an infinite series of interpretations, but there might be many. Derrida has complained that his famous dictum 'there is nothing outside the text' has been seriously misunderstood. If all human life and systems form a discourse, a text, then meaning is to be found within it. We cannot stand outside it; it is a

Societies have different values, which are shown in customs and taboos. Where do these come from? They are not part of the 'deep structures' of language.

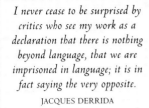

I never cease to be surprised by critics who see my work as a declaration that there is nothing beyond language, that we are imprisoned in language; it is in fact saying the very opposite.

JACQUES DERRIDA

Human beings are creative and imaginative, expressing individual and new ideas, or forming great art or music.

self-enclosed dialogue where each sign refers to another within the system. Derrida speaks of the trace of ideas interwoven in any text. They are not always self-evidently present, but reference to them is implied. There is an external reality, though, that we respond to and form language to deal with. This is a vital point for our later discussion of theology.

Facing reality

The arbitrariness of the signs may also have been overemphasized. When Barthes argued that traffic lights could have used any series of colours, he was ignoring the facts of nature – some colours are more visible and distinctive to the human eye than others. Likewise, hitting the deck with the flat of the hand for a

wrestler is physically easier than singing a song when tired out and hurting all over! We are restricted in the signs we can employ. A wrestler might dream of flying over the ring to show that he has given up, but that is all. We are limited by the world around us; we only create a sense of reality in our minds up to a point.

Summing up

Language is a human creation and cannot have direct access to reality or make it present to us. There is an absence, a distance of interpretation – words and discourses can contain many different levels of meaning. Deconstruction unveils the many possible meanings and the hidden agendas and unconscious aspects of a text.

63

THE SELF

What is the 'self' that we sense in our heads? This is often referred to as the *cogito*: the 'I think' or the thinking subject.

Earlier generations had no doubt that there was a spirit, a vital force, inhabiting the body. Neanderthal burial sites in Iraq show that they believed in an afterlife. The body was curled up in the foetal position as if ready for rebirth, with red dye and flowers placed over it.

The Greek philosophers speculated that the soul was made up of various elements, some of which belonged to the lower order of the body, and some to the higher, spiritual realm. Reason was higher and survived the death of

the body; the emotions and will were lower and did not. Popular beliefs were many and varied, though, ranging from the transmigration of souls (reincarnation) to survival as a ghost in the underworld.

Hebrew thought was more suggestive and elusive. The self was the soul or the spirit or even the heart, which was seen as the seat of the emotions, a vital part of the self. There was not such a distinction made between soul and body. The self was more than the spirit or vital force, which animated the body. It was the whole. This holistic vision resulted in various doctrines of resurrection, of rising again into the fullness of life with some kind of form or body.

The idea of a soul in a body was at the heart of most thinking about the self until the empiricists doubted the existence of anything immaterial. Postmodern thought has inadvertently re-evaluated the idea of a soul.

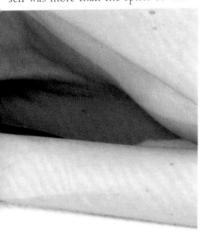

Contents

You will not abandon me to the grave . . .
You have made known to me the path of life;
you will fill me with joy in your presence,
with eternal pleasures at your right hand.

PSALM 16:10–11

Freud and Psychoanalysis

The Enlightenment began with a firm belief in an immortal soul, but the rising influence of the empiricists led people to question anything that could not be measured by physical means. As the idea of God was rejected, the existence of the soul was cast into doubt as well.

The Austrian psychiatrist Sigmund Freud (1856–1939) lived in Vienna for much of his life. He worked within the milieu of modernism, but some of his insights were explosive and deconstructive. They have been developed in a postmodern manner by succeeding thinkers, but Freud began the deconstruction of the self.

Freud developed the free-association technique, where he let the patient speak freely, even ramble, lying on a couch. He believed that the stories and ramblings would eventually lead him to the root of the problem. Painful memories were resisted. Patients came at them indirectly, because they did not want to face up to them at first. Freud's free-association method included the retelling of memorable dreams; for him they were an important resource. Freud published *The Interpretation of Dreams* in 1900. Dreams could reveal deep feelings in coded form.

Conscience is the internal perception of the rejection of a particular wish operating within us.

SIGMUND FREUD, TOTEM AND TABOO

The unconscious

Freud mapped out the human mind in a new way. The dominant idea about human

Oedipus Solving the Riddles of the Sphinx (1808) by Jean Auguste Dominque Ingres (1780–1867).

Sigmund Freud reading the manuscript of *An Outline of Psychoanalysis*.

The unconscious was irrational, and concerned with deep drives, particularly the sex drive and the need to procreate. He spoke of this energy as 'libido' and the sexual instinct as 'the pleasure principle'. The human psyche strove to find balance and maturity, to form relationships with others so that we could mate and produce children. There was a dynamic of life versus death within us, a drive to preserve the race.

Id, superego and ego

In-between the ego and the id (Latin for 'it' and a term of reference for the uncharted seas of the unconscious) is the superego. This is an internalization of the Father, of his will and rule, censoring impulses and desires that are disapproved of by the child's own father and/or the mores and norms of the prevailing society. Freud took this idea from the myth of Oedipus: Oedipus killed his own father unknowingly and slept with his mother, Jocasta.

consciousness had been reason. Freud's work with his patients led him to form the idea of the unconscious, a deep level of the mind beneath conscious thoughts. He saw consciousness as the tip of the iceberg, and also spoke of the preconscious – ideas and feelings that could be expressed in conscious thought. The unconscious was deeper and more mysterious. Feelings and energy from the unconscious had to surface and pass into the preconscious and then the conscious before they could be faced and understood.

Freud and the Self

The new discipline of psychoanalysis shattered the presuppositions of society and opened up radical new ways of analysing the self.

Freud's unconscious was a deep well of darkness where silence ruled. It was preliterate and preconceptual – chaotic. The personal subject was an autonomous ego who learned how to use language, which existed 'out there' as a social convention. As we learned how to speak, so we could begin to understand the unconscious in fragments. Its drives could be glimpsed in dream symbols and suppressed desires. It dealt with libido – sex drive – the bare will to procreate and survive.

The narcissistic stage

Freud saw desire as selfish, as the desire to possess the other and to be at the centre of our existence. We could easily become locked in the narcissistic stage (Freud's reference to the Greek myth of Narcissus, who fell in love with his own reflection). We needed to learn how to form relationships with give and take, to be socialized, to live a more balanced life, and to form loving sexual relationships.

In conclusion

Freud ultimately had a negative sense of the self. At root it was a formless, silent, chaotic sea

of desires that needed to be tamed by the censorious ego. The goal of mental health, the reason for psychotherapy, was to provide balance and allow sexual relationships to happen. But once procreation had been achieved, there was no inner goal for the latter half of life.

Though Freud overturned the Greek elevation of reason, ironically he colluded with it, for reason was still master and everything else had to be kept in check. The self was somehow just there, socialized in stages but all there within. He was sceptical about an afterlife, seeing this as a form of wish fulfilment – we cannot face the idea of dying, and thus we create imaginary fantasies as soothing consolations.

Narcissus by Michelangelo Merisi da Caravaggio (1570–1610).

> *The psychic development of the individual is a short repetition of the course of development of the race.*
>
> SIGMUND FREUD,
> 'LEONARDO DA VINCI AND A MEMORY OF HIS CHILDHOOD'

THE COMB

One of Freud's patients was a Jewish woman who had a dream of a strange man handing her a comb. Using free association, Freud searched for a clue. The young woman had been asked by a Gentile who was very much in love with her to marry him. She did not feel that she could marry a non-Jew – what about bringing up the children?

The comb suddenly made sense when she spoke of an argument she had had with her mother just before the dream, and she had thought of leaving home. Further probing recalled a childhood scolding for using a stranger's comb: 'You'll mix the breed!' The comb was a cipher for mixed-race relations, and the stranger was the lover.

Here, we can see the manifest content of a dream, and the latent content. The latent content was the fear of disapproval for mixing races. Dream symbols can thus be displacements of deeper feelings and anxieties.

Carl Gustav Jung

Freud's pupils developed his thought. The most significant work was achieved by the Swiss psychoanalyst Carl Gustav Jung (1875–1961).

Jung broke with Freud over the interpretation of dreams, and worked out a different theory of the unconscious. He was to give symbols, mystery, spirit and the unspeakable a central role in human life. This rediscovery of the enigmatic, incomplete and poetic is a key aspect of postmodernism. Jung began to notice that his patients had dreams and fantasies that paralleled some of the symbolism he had studied in mythology and comparative religion.

The collective unconscious

These experiences gradually led to Jung's theory of the collective unconscious – the human unconscious was not

> *Among all my patients in the second half of life... there has not been one whose problem in the last resort was not that of finding a religious view of life.*
>
> CARL GUSTAV JUNG,
> *MODERN MAN IN SEARCH OF A SOUL*

just a wild, immoral dustbin as in Freud's id, but a repository of many ancient forces, symbols and wisdom. He saw the unconscious as being a largely positive force that worked for the harmony of the individual – repressed emotions fed the shadow self, but there was more

Psychoanalyst Carl Gustav Jung on the cover of *Time* magazine, February 1955.

in the unconscious than darkness. 'Mental illness' could therefore be seen as an escalated programme of psychological growth and healing – feelings were released and visions and potent symbols reared up that

THE AZTEC AND THE VOLCANO

A woman reported a dream of an Aztec warrior riding on a horse. A snake bites him and then bites and kills the horse. An earthquake shakes the ground and a volcano erupts. The Aztec is engulfed in the landslide.

Jung interpreted this as her need to be free of her dominant mother; if her psyche could not be independent, then she would be 'buried' under the landslide of emotions and would have a breakdown. The Aztec is her deepest self.

tap into, the Self being the circumference of a circle, at the centre of which stands the self.

The concept of the Self as the deepest layer of our being has been taken over in various schools of therapy. New Age mysticism has claimed the term for our spiritual nature, and, by borrowing from Eastern thought, has declared the Self to be part of God.

Who are we, then?

Jung allowed the unconscious to be fundamentally purposive and positive, seeing a drive towards integration and inner peace in old age. Life was not all about procreation. Yet what we are is a mystery with Jung. He plays with the concept of the persona, a word meaning 'actor's mask' in the Greek. We wear different masks, try on different roles for different people and situations. Who is the real 'me'?

helped to draw the psyche together.

Jung believed that the conscious self was part of a much bigger whole, and he spoke of the Self and the self. The Self was seen as the collective experience of humanity that we can all

Jacques Lacan

Jacques Lacan (1901–81) developed Freud's thought. He was particularly interested in the work of the surrealists and their use of symbolism. He brought semiotics and structuralism into the study of the human psyche.

Lacan tried to establish the structure of the psyche and to see this in terms of signs and signifiers. He related psychoanalysis to semiotics, and described the self as embedded in the flow of language. His work has influenced a number of postmodern thinkers.

The mirror and the symbolic
Lacan saw the ego as a false unity, or as an 'envelope' that covered the diverse parts of the body. In infanthood, the self has little control over the body and its functions. The ego is formed by fixing upon an image outside itself. This might be a reflection in a mirror, or another infant. This gives a sense of wholeness that compensates for the undeveloped motor coordination of the body. This is the mirror phase.

Besides this image, there is the influence of the social world into which the child is born, and the stream of signifiers that are spoken and indicated around it. Language

pre-dates the ego in this sense, in the community. Expectations, statements of affirmation or punishment, comparisons with relatives and so forth, form a world of meaning in which the child finds a sense of identity and belonging. This is the symbolic phase. Image is combined with words and names.

Ideals and egos
Lacan spoke of identification with the ideal, by which he

For Lacan, the image-from-the-mirror phase fades as children grow up, changing to a sense of self, constructed from the outside and from others.

meant a figure spoken into the child's life by its community. The ideal might be a parent or grandparent, or an older brother, for example. This is part of the complex mechanism known as the ego, and might give the child a tendency to repeat the mistakes of an ancestor. This

Lacan, attacking Descartes and the idea of a fixed self, the thinking subject (or *cogito*), wrote that the mirror stage was useful:

for the light it sheds on the formation of the 'I' as we experience it in psychoanalysis. It is an experience that leads us to oppose any philosophy directly issuing from the cogito.

JACQUES LACAN,
ÉCRITS

Jacques Lacan developed the work of Freud.

ideal identification is rooted in the mirror phase.

Lacan saw the image from the mirror phase as relinquishing its grip as the child grew into adulthood. The child's place in society came by moving more into the world of the symbolic, and out into a wider field of symbols and references outside the family and local community. The symbolic would become more influential.

Our sense of self is thus constructed from the outside; we learn who we are from others. Therefore, Lacan could speak of the ideal ego and the ego ideal. The ideal ego is the original image of yourself formed in infancy, and the ego ideal is the idea of yourself formed by the wider social, symbolic order. This challenges us with an idea of what we are expected to be. You might have an image of yourself as a shy introvert, but who is this image for? Who or what has helped to programme this into your psyche?

The Self as a Sign?

How true is it that the self is a fiction itself? Is it no more than a sign, an illusion of sorts?

Lacan spoke of the ego as imaginary because this was a false unifying concept, which ignored the deeper unconscious built up from the symbolic realm. Freud said that the ego censors the unconscious, just like two subjects at work in the same psyche. Lacan saw the unconscious as being structured like a language, and in this he followed the logic of structuralist linguistics: the self is itself a sign, a social construct. He seems to be saying that everything is put into us from outside. We are a product of all these signifiers and images.

The real

Lacan left open the possibility for something to exist that was not signified. He spoke of the category of the real, meaning that which is not or cannot be

I think where I am not, therefore I am where I do not think. Is what thinks in my place, then, another I?

JACQUES LACAN,
ATTACKING THE CARTESIAN,
UNIFIED *COGITO* IN THE
LIGHT OF PSYCHOANALYSIS

symbolized. There are things excluded from our symbolic systems, on the margins, subconsciously ignored, or that defy conceptualization. It is rather like the tourist in Soviet Russia who asked about a church across the street from their tour group. The communist guide replied, 'That is not on my map!' Maybe, just maybe, there is something in the psyche that cannot be traced to external influences.

A satisfying synthesis

Julia Kristeva was a pupil of Lacan, but she has developed his thought in new directions. In her Marxist training in Bulgaria, Kristeva was schooled in the dialectical argument of Georg Hegel (1770–1831). Freud had the thesis of the completely autonomous

HEGEL'S DIALECTICS

Hegel taught that a thesis presented with an antithesis could produce a synthesis, a harmonization of the conflicting opinions.

Julia Kristeva, one-time pupil of Lacan who has taken his thinking in new directions.

subject; Lacan the antithesis of the completely socially structured subject; Kristeva had the synthesis of an active, actual subject that was partly formed by society and was in the process of becoming.

Is everything poured into us from outside to form a sense of self? Or is it there to some degree already?

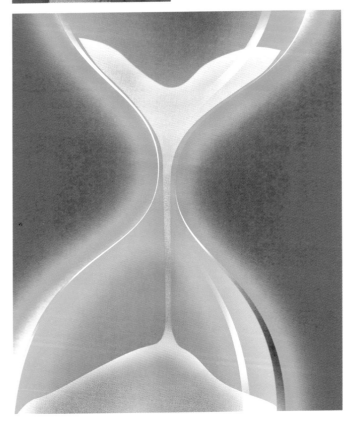

The Deterritorialized Self

The work of Deleuze and Guattari spun new concepts and broke open our patterns of thought to allow the new, the intriguing and the 'monstrous'.

The French philosophers Gilles Deleuze (1925–95) and Felix Guattari (1930–92) worked together on some conceptually radical volumes, including *Anti-Oedipus* and *A Thousand Plateaus*. They attack modernism constantly for its dominance and its attempt to systematize and control thought, the self, emotions and the body. They seek to overthrow Freudian psychoanalysis, for this is defined by capitalism. The sense of ego and self, the role of the family and resulting taboos and inhibitions are economically defined by the consumer society, which relies upon forms of stable family units. They link the Oedipal individual, with his or her complexes and repressed desires, to the state, which becomes the Father, in Freudian terms.

> *To open us up to the inhuman and the overhuman… to go beyond the human condition is the meaning of philosophy…*
>
> GILLES DELEUZE,
> *BERGSONISM*

Desiring machines

The self should be rediscovered and configured according to libidinal impulses or desire. Desire itself is revolutionary. Society seeks to hem it in, to control and repress it. Deleuze and Guattari call this 'territorializing'. Society is only possible at the expense of individual freedom. As they say in *Anti-Oedipus*, 'To code desire is the business of society.'

Codification is to be broken and diversified. There can be many codes and systems, not just one. Bodies are 'desiring machines', as machines connect flows and can arrange and rearrange them. The individual's libido is preconscious and pre-Oedipal. It is channelled and dammed up in various ways by various regimes.

They coined the term 'schizoanalysis' to challenge these structures of domination; they seek to open up the flow of the unconscious, enabling us to leave the restrictive ego and superego behind. 'Deterritorializing the body' seeks to free it of socially articulated models and self-images.

Roots and connections, not trees

They spurn the hierarchical idea of trees of knowledge, with layers of subjects or historical epochs, one upon another. They seek to look at roots, at deep structures and influences, and they move across epochs, up and down tables and trees, to make ad hoc and varied connections between times, places, people and concepts. This is the idea of the nomad, the drifting thinker who never seeks to complete his or her thought, but simply goes on and on thinking and questing. Nomads of desire seek to live untrammelled by rules and codes of domination.

Mere specks

Deleuze and Guattari try to move beyond the human or the anthropomorphic to break down our culture of dominance. They remind us that humans are a mere speck in the history of biological life, and the mineral and the artificial (silicon) world can be a bearer of 'overhuman' forms of intelligence in the future – supercomputers and artificial intelligence. What is coming?

Humans as desiring machines. Who are we? What are our limits? Who says?

77

The History of a Self

The idea of the self has a history, being appreciated and defined differently in different ages. What do we mean by 'I' and has it any actual, quantifiable reality?

The French post-structuralist Michel Foucault followed the view that the self is a fiction, a construct that evolves and shifts. It has a history. Foucault was concerned with the 'archaeology' of truth, the social and cultural influences that have helped to form opinions. The sense of self has its own history or archaeology in layers of influences in family and society, and also in epochs of history. The sense of the self before Descartes and his '*Cogito, ergo sum*' ('I think, therefore I am') was different. He provided a model that saw the self as an inner essence in the body. Now we see the self as a psychological construct (at least up to a point), in close harmony with the body and environment.

According to Foucault, the idea of the self is constantly reinvented and rewritten, sometimes as a member of a community in more traditional societies, sometimes as a

The I, the I is what is deeply mysterious.

LUDWIG
WITTGENSTEIN,
NOTEBOOKS

distinct individual, sometimes as spirit and body, sometimes as psychosomatic unity, sometimes as a cluster of experiences and psychological drives. It just goes on and on.

'I' is not 'me'

The Viennese philosopher Ludwig Wittgenstein (1889–1951) teased out ideas of the self with his linguistic analyses. One commentator has pointed out that each page of one of his major works contains eight references to 'I'. He was concerned that we fall under the spell of language, thinking unclearly and believing all kinds of illusions. If I say that I have failed at something, then, grammatically, I am reporting a series of facts. 'I' can only equal the failure if 'I' is seen as an objective entity in my head. We might work out our identities through various means – ID cards, fingerprints and so on. What is the real self that I sense? The danger is to fix this

Foucault practised Zen Buddhism in later life, with its maxim, 'I'm no one going nowhere.' Its attempt to strip the ego of illusions suited his scepticism. Perhaps he was a subject in search of a self. As he once said, 'Do not ask me who I am and do not ask me to remain the same.'

What is the 'I' that feels joy? Where is the joy?

in an essence that cannot be defined. 'I' is not 'me' the object, the bunch of facts and details; 'I' is more fluid and spontaneous. Even a person with amnesia speaks of themselves as 'I' – 'I have lost my memory.'

Joy was one example used by Wittgenstein. We might show joy in our facial expressions, or feel it inside. It is very real, but not quantifiable or able to be

localized. It is 'no thing' in this sense.

Losing and Finding Yourself

The paradox is that the more we give, the more we receive. We cannot form relationships without giving freely to 'the other'.

Kristeva has commented that the subject's finding of itself is a paradox, for it is only in giving up something of self to relate to another that we find ourselves.

Desire is not merely narcissistic; it is a response to a call from the other. Postmodernism often uses the term 'the other' or 'Other', sometimes designating this alterity. There is a deep and profound sense that existence is relational, and a human being, the very idea of a self, cannot be defined in isolation. Desire with Freud and Lacan was self-centred, seeking self-needs and affirmation. Lacan linked it with the adherence to the 'ideal'.

Kristeva goes beyond these categories and frees the self to genuinely relate. There is a wholesome dynamic. She tries to recreate the old values and depths of the inner life as experienced in the framework of Christian faith without the faith – the power of love and self-worth, being loved by the other for what we are and brought to fulfilment. She rejects an empty, cynical reductionism and nihilism.

For whoever wants to save his life will lose it, but whoever loses his life for me and for the gospel will save it.

JESUS, MARK 8:35

Strangers to ourselves

Kristeva, as an immigrant into French society from Bulgaria, has written a study of attitudes to foreigners and strangers in history. *Strangers to Ourselves* is about the émigré, the absolute quintessence of French chic from one angle, but someone who cannot help but feel an outsider within. Kristeva is passionately involved in SOS Racisme, campaigning against racism.

She ends her study of foreignness by referring to the stranger within each of us, the strangeness of the unconscious. Freud has spoken of the 'uncanny strangeness' we feel when confronted with certain issues, symbols or people – a surfacing of what

Not belonging to any place, any time, any love. A lost origin, the impossibility to take root, a rummaging memory, the present in abeyance. The space of the foreigner is a moving train, a plane in flight, the very transition that precludes stopping. As to landmarks, there are none. His time? The time of a resurrection that remembers death and what happened before, but misses the glory of being beyond: merely the feeling of a reprieve, of having gotten away.

JULIA KRISTEVA
STRANGERS TO OURSELVES

Desire is a response to a call from the other. *The Kiss* by Gustav Klimt (1862–1918).

we have excluded and repressed. The xenophobe projects all that he or she fears onto a stranger, a kind of anti-ideal, a narcissistic doppelganger who repels rather than enthrals. Jung spoke of the shadow self, where all our fears and hatred were projected.

There is an uncanny strangeness within all of us; we are strangers to ourselves. When we recognize this, Kristeva asks, 'Might not universality be… our own foreignness?' She speaks of the healing power of welcome and meeting: 'Meeting balances wandering. A crossroads of two othernesses, it welcomes the foreigner without tying him down, opening the host to his visitor without committing him.'

81

Nothing Stranger Than the Self

Strangeness, otherness and mystery are vital components of the self. We need a holistic mode, not a reductionist one — and what of the soul?

Kristeva's concept of the stranger within is evocative. There is something that cannot be defined and catalogued within the psyche. Postmodernism plays with the mysterious and the negative spaces. We cannot define the self even after all our semiotic endeavours. It is partly a structure derived from language and culture around us. But there is something that responds, something that can be shaped and evolved as a given. The self is at root a gift.

Consciousness?

Lacan saw the self as an assembly of many aspects and influences all working together, rather like a university — this is a unifying concept for a mass of people, departments and buildings. If the self is 'no thing', it is still conscious. The whole is finally greater than the sum of the parts, special, precious and mysterious. Consciousness is the final mystery of neurological studies. It cannot be traced to any part of the brain, but is a function of the whole organism.

Mind/body

We are back to where we began. Does postmodernism help us with the mind/body problem? Can we believe in a life after death any more? Postmodern philosophers have not dealt with this directly, and their own theistic beliefs vary. In popular discourse, two options are presented:

◆ The mind is no more than a product of a living brain.

Is the self an amalgamation of various drives and influences?

If we cannot say for sure that we can survive the death of the body, then can we trust that we might?

◆ The brain is like a TV set that the soul tunes into.

In postmodernism, the two opposed models can give way to a third, more open option:

◆ The mind is partly produced by the working brain and social influences, but it is also a deeply mysterious thing, conscious and alive.

The issue is philosophically undecidable. The mind can be seen as a by-product of the brain from one angle, and as a mysterious essence from another. It is like light existing both as waves and as particles in different situations. There is that which is beyond the rational in us, and we should not be surprised if we cannot solve all mysteries by the power of reason. The nature of the self is left as an open question. A postmodernist would shun traditional metaphysics and admit how much we cannot know. In that absence, that gap, that *aporia* of knowledge, there might be room for faith, faith as trust and not as sure knowledge.

Summing up

The self has many levels, both conscious and unconscious, as revealed in psychoanalysis and in ancient beliefs. We have hidden depths, and society can help to fashion a sense of self-identity with its norms, pressures and symbolic order. We define ourselves in relation to the other.

THE FEMININE

A band of women was on the march in Paris on International Women's Day, 8 March 1968, carrying placards reading, 'Down with feminism'. They did not want a return to traditional values; they were all socially aware and militant in their own way. These women were reacting to a form of feminism that sought to neutralize gender differences in a bland drive towards equality. They were part of the emerging philosophy of postmodernism, allying themselves with key thinkers such as Derrida, and using postmodern terms to elucidate the difference between the sexes.

Antoinette Fouque, a lecturer at the University of Paris VIII, Vincennes, and a member of Psych et po (*psychanalyse et*

An early feminist demonstration.

politique), formed a publishing group in 1970: Des femmes. Fouque, now an MEP, was concerned with identity, not just equality. Feminine identity did not mean 'sameness' with maleness. Des femmes established a style of writing – *écriture féminine* – to help women articulate their experience and their feelings. Centuries of patriarchal culture had shaped concepts and repressed feminine types of thinking and feeling.

A key writer is Hélène Cixous, Professor of English at Vincennes, whose writing is deliberately non-linear and poetic. In her view, the feminist movement masculinizes women, bringing them into patriarchal, bourgeois power structures that need rethinking, whereas expressing repressed femininity collapses binary opposition, logocentrism and other masculine forms of control and hierarchy. She speaks of 'writing the body' and 'text as tissue', stressing the immanent, the earthly and the bodily, not the remote, abstract and coolly rational.

Contents

Let's go to the school of writing, where we'll spend three school days initiating ourselves in the strange science of writing, which is a science of farewells. Of reunitings.
I shall begin with: H
This is what writing is.

HÉLÈNE CIXOUS,
THREE STEPS ON THE LADDER OF WRITING

What is a Woman?

The Psych et po movement is sometimes described as postfeminist, as it moves beyond classical feminism. It recognizes the struggle for rights, but raises questions about gender that some feminists tend to ignore.

Feminists reject the notion of biological essentialism. This is the idea that the nature of men and women is fixed at birth, and that the feminine is passively subordinate to the thrusting, creative, rational masculine. Simone de Beauvoir (1908–86) articulated this position in *The Second Sex* in 1949. This French thinker and partner of Jean-Paul Sartre used existentialism to show that women can be free to choose who they want to be: 'One is not born, but rather becomes, a woman.' They need to escape the social construction of the feminine as innately passive and selfless, a construct that suits patriarchal assumptions and aspirations.

Postfeminists argue that there is something given at birth; human beings are sexed – engendered – and this difference needs to be explored in a free and open way. They must have

Feminist writer Simone de Beauvoir.

the same rights, but they are different. The feminine is the other to the masculine, and vice versa. Postfeminism states that what a woman is has not yet emerged or really been understood. Feminists react against patriarchy, but have rubbed out their own distinctive nature in the process.

Psychoanalysis

On the question of biological essentialism, Sigmund Freud is an ambivalent figure for women. Many feminists reject

Certain modern tendencies, certain feminists of our time, make strident demands for sex to be neutralized. This neutralization, if it were possible, would mean the end of the human species. The human species is divided into two genders which ensure its production and reproduction. To wish to get rid of sexual difference is to call for a genocide more radical than any form of destruction there has ever been in history.

LUCE IRIGARAY,
JE, TU, NOUS – *TOWARD A CULTURE OF DIFFERENCE*

his method of psychoanalysis as they fear it reinforces patriarchy. Others see the beginning of a recognition of the distinctively feminine, and attempt to assess their characters and needs.

Freud rescued women from the curse of hysteria. In the 19th century, hysteria was thought to be a physical complaint, attached to the uterus and the ovaries (from the Greek *hysteros*: 'womb'). It was seen as an exclusively feminine complaint. Freud debunked this idea, showing how hysterical symptoms were the result of repressed emotions and neuroses.

Equal but different? The *Temptation of Adam* by the Master of Lucretia, 16th century.

Penis Envy

Postfeminists have been influenced by psychoanalysis and the revelations it brings of deep, often hidden, human drives and emotions.

Some key postfeminist thinkers have undergone psychoanalysis or are practising analysts themselves, though they reject some key ideas deriving from Freud.

Freud probed into sexuality and repression, believing that there was a forgotten story of sexuality that had to be recovered from our infancy. He used a mythical story to frame this, that of Oedipus, who sleeps with his own mother and finds that he has killed his own father. Boys develop wanting the mother, but distance themselves from her as they fear castration by the dominant father. Girls realize their lack of a penis, and turn from the mother to the father figure for completion. The desire for a penis is translated into the desire to bear children and is known as 'penis envy' in Freudian psychoanalysis. Thus, sexuality is defined by the phallic. Obviously, this stance is awkward for feminists and postfeminists alike.

The male subject possesses the penis but he does not have access to the phallus.

JACQUES LACAN, *ÉCRITS*

Lacan

Jacques Lacan has had a direct influence upon postfeminist thinkers. Antoinette Fouque underwent therapy from him, and the writers Luce Irigaray and Julia Kristeva were his pupils. His linguistic model of the unconscious, with the three stages of the imaginary, the real and the symbolic, opened up psychoanalysis to the world of structuralist thought and semiotics. The infant believes itself to be part of the mother in the real; the ego starts to

The great question, which I have not been able to answer, despite my thirty years of research into the feminine soul, is 'What does a woman want?'

SIGMUND FREUD

form as it recognizes itself in a reflection or another child in the imaginary; and the self-conscious 'self' enters the symbolic order of language and becomes reflexive in the symbolic. Language is about lack or loss – a loss of identification with the mother.

Lacan gave Freud's concept of penis envy a new spin. The infant male recognizes that the phallus separates him from the mother in the imaginary phase; the phallus is linked with the appropriation of language in the symbolic phase, as this is only possible with a sense of self, distance and loss. The phallus takes on a new and deeper symbolic meaning that is not just about the male, biological penis. It is an archetypal idea. Naturally, some women have reacted against the phallus as the main symbol of difference and lack.

The phallus is not to be reduced to the biological penis. It is a symbol of loss. *David* by Michelangelo Buonarroti (1475–1564).

Jungian Archetypes

Jung developed Freud's thinking in a different direction from Lacan. His insights into the symbolic order opened up deeper mysteries about male/female identity.

Jung was open to playful images and the power of symbols. He anticipated aspects of postmodernism, seeing other forms of discourse as valid as well as the rational. The archetypal symbols for Jung were potent, inherited symbols that revealed aspects of the truth about ourselves. There are numerous potent symbols, and that of the anima/animus has a bearing upon feminism and postfeminism.

Anima/animus

Jung argued that a man has an inner self-image that is feminine in symbolic form, and a woman has a male image. These are the anima and the animus. Hence, one of his patients imagined herself as an Aztec warrior in a dream.

Jung thought that poor relationships with the opposite sex would make the soul image distorted and extreme. A man might see women as oppressive if he had a dominant mother, or as wanton harlots if he was emotionally repressed. In a woman, an extreme, controlling dictator figure could form.

Sometimes the anima/animus is the internalized idea of the opposite sex, and can function as a symbol of 'the Self' in Jung. He said that he had conversed with his own anima many times in dreams, and this opened the door into his unconscious self. This also

A man with a fear of women might see his anima as a seductress.

Jung had a vivid dream in 1913 of buildings being engulfed by chaotic floods. He saw the outbreak of the First World War a year later as its fulfilment or correspondence in external reality.

acknowledged that there is a 'feminine' streak in a man and vice versa in a woman. Macho culture represses the anima, hiding feelings and stunting the ability to express them – 'Boys don't cry!' The feminine is denied access to powers of logic and control.

Sexist stereotyping?

Jung has helped to liberate both men and women to recognize something of the other in themselves. Men and women are not so different, after all. Men are scared of their feelings, and so they

A powerful, dominating animus can make a woman seem more 'masculine'.

As far as we can discern, the sole purpose of human existence is to kindle a light in the darkness of mere being.

CARL GUSTAV JUNG, *MEMORIES, DREAMS, REFLECTIONS*

subjugate women. Wherein lies the difference between the genders? The perennial problem is how much to assign to nature, and how much to assign to nurture. Some things might be given at birth, but our identities are also socially constructed, up to a point. The repressed feminine wants to speak, and in hearing her voice we might all find ourselves.

Jung's insistence upon the role of psychic health and individuation (personal harmony and integration) in the latter half of life, irrespective of the power to procreate, has opened up a respect and a search for spirituality, for wholeness, meaning and interiority. This has captivated postmodernists. Postfeminists, who are attuned to bodily rhythm, the mother, and the power of creativity, perhaps find this even more attractive.

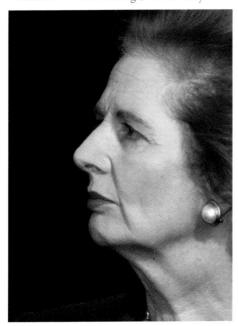

Deconstructing the Feminine

Derrida's tactic of deconstruction has opened up new possibilities for postfeminist critics to analyse Western culture and the role of women.

Deconstruction exposes the conscious and unconscious influences at work in a text, and seeks to counter the dominant, Western stance of working with binary opposition. Derrida demonstrated how a pair of opposites always ends up with one being privileged over the other, such as men/women. He asks us to think what the difference would be if the second term came first.

Derrida also attacks the assumption that speech is to be preferred to writing. The former is seen as purer and fresher, and the latter as a second-hand relic of a conversation. His playful term '*différance*' works to undermine this, as it is a mutant term, created by him, that can only be recognized when written. It sounds the same as 'difference' in speech and thus loses its meaning. Hence, he privileges writing over speech!

His attack on logocentrism not only questions the possibility of forming a sure, foundational model of knowledge, but it also overturns the Western, rational scheme whereby certain forms of expression are repressed and sidelined. That which cannot be spoken, that which can only be felt, or at best evoked by words stretched playfully and poetically, also has its place. The feminine perspective is one

such repressed *épistème*: women have been 'under erasure', as he would put it.

Logocentrism and the phallus

Postfeminists have attacked Lacan's use of the phallus as the primary signifier in Western thought, seeing this as a classic case of binary opposition and logocentrism. *Logos* (reason) and the phallus

Love is the time and space where 'I' give myself the right to be extraordinary.

JULIA KRISTEVA,
TALES OF LOVE

are linked as the rational, 'male' principle. What has been placed 'under erasure' or underprivileged in the discourse? Western thought is thus exposed as being phallocentric.

Tel Quel

The late sixties saw the rise of the *Tel Quel* group, intellectuals who contributed to the avant-garde literary journal *Tel Quel*, and were involved in the run up to, and the aftermath of, the events of May 1968 – the large-scale student riots and workers' march in Paris. Derrida was involved, along with members of Psych et po. Julia Kristeva, for example, married the journal's editor, Phillipe Sollers. There was interplay and cross-fertilization of ideas. The feminine and its need for a discourse was developing alongside the foundations of postmodern thought and post-structuralism.

'Woman as such does not exist. She is in the process of becoming' (Julia Kristeva).

Luce Irigaray

Luce Irigaray is a prominent and original French postfeminist thinker and practising analyst. She seeks to rethink the superstructure of Western philosophy.

Irigaray was born in Belgium in 1932, and has worked at the Centre National de Recherches Scientifiques in Paris since 1974. She is now Director of Research in Philosophy. She studied under Lacan at the École Freudienne, and worked with schizophrenic clients whom she believed were overwhelmed by language and were unable to construct a self-image. Irigaray believed this was particularly true of women – the male-dominated language of our concepts had smothered their inner resources. This began her drive to rethink philosophy, which culminated in her work *Speculum of the Other Woman* in 1974. Lacan fell out with her over this.

The sexed subject

Irigaray questions the 'master discourse' of Western philosophy, which seeks to see the subject or consciousness as sexually neutral as it transcends the body and the physical. This is the Cartesian fallacy and she rethinks philosophy in terms of the male and the female subject.

She rejects Lacan's phallocentric theory, and Freud's notion of penis envy. Psychoanalysis is too patriarchal at root and has ignored the maternal and the feminine. She speaks of 'the

THE CAVE

In Plato's *Republic*, he tells the famous parable of the cave. People sit inside the cave watching shadows cast onto the cave walls by sunlight, which shines through the entrance behind them. They live in unreality, but when one turns and looks towards the source of the light, and climbs out into the world above, then he sees with truth, reason and clarity.

In *Speculum*, Irigaray interrogates and deconstructs this text. The cave is the womb, and the shadows are the dark space and the immanent experiences of everyday life. The climb away is the separation of the ego from the mother, and the self-image that results is based upon a repudiation of the maternal.

Luce Irigaray was expelled from the École Freudienne at Vincennes in 1974 after she departed from Lacan's phallocentric teaching.

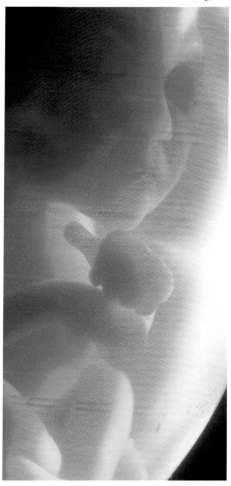

The 'hole' need not be lack, but is a place of creation.

murder of the mother' in Western culture as women are placed 'under erasure'. The maternal/feminine is unrecognized and invisible in discourse because the real difference is not acknowledged and allowed to be in the symbolic realm. She seeks to 'interrogate the philosophical tradition'.

In Lacan's thought, women present us with a 'hole' and not a penis. In Irigaray's thought, this need not be defined as lack, but positive space and creative mystery. Her reference to a speculum, a small mirror for peeking inside the body, refers to the need to look inside the 'hole' and see things as they are specific to women. She writes poetically and playfully, following the *écriture féminine* of Hélène Cixous. The 'hole' becomes a passageway to the dark continent, noting that in psychoanalysis, women are treated as colonized territory. Just as Western values were imposed upon African tribal groups, so women are trampled under masculine terms and concerns. This dark space is mysterious but not to be feared. It is the place of creation, or conception and pregnancy, rich and glorious.

The 'hole' is an O, a circle – a sense of completion, not of lack. The 'hole' speaks of the whole, of a holistic vision of life.

Julia Kristeva

Kristeva works in the fields of linguistics and psychoanalysis, and has rethought aspects of Freud and Lacan's systems. She points us back to the preverbal zone of awareness in infancy that we regress to under extreme mental disturbance.

Kristeva was born in Bulgaria in 1941, and she travelled to Paris in 1966, having studied semiotics and Marxist philosophy. She is a teacher of philosophy and semiotics, as well as a practising analyst. She disowns the name 'feminist' (which she often writes in inverted commas) as this denotes, for her, an attempt to find power in conceptually flawed existing frameworks that do not recognize the place and value of the maternal. Thus, she is very much a part of Psych et po. She does continue to work within the framework of Freudian and Lacanian psychoanalysis, but disrupts

THE CHORA

Plato's *Timaeus* speculates about the existence of a mysterious, undefinable, womb-like space, which exists prior to any idea of forms in the creation of the cosmos: the *chora*. Kristeva relocates this within each of us as the deep well of life, the maternal, pre-Oedipal impulses. It is the shared space of mother and child. This poetic form of awareness allows paradox to come into play, whereas binary opposition always rejects and opposes the other. Things can be both/and. The *chora* lives on as desire and as expressions in music, art and poetry. As this resists rational and logical representation, it disrupts the dominance of patriarchy.

The *chora* is somewhat repressed as we enter the symbolic order, but there are *aporias*, slippages, forgetful moments, in ecstacy, awe, poetry and musical rhythm. Science ignores this realm and speaks as though it does not exist. Thus, science is incomplete and truncated. The semiotic stage or level is disruptive of the symbolic order; it precedes it and cannot be totally regulated by it. However, it also depends upon it to function in society.

these systems at various points. She has even spoken of 'feminists' as hysterics (using this in Freudian terms). Hysteria is the result of a disjointed lack of balance and self-centring; women are hysterics because they are caught up in a patriarchal discourse where they are defined by lack.

The semiotic

For the Swiss linguist Saussure, the semiotic meant a system of signs, but Kristeva redefines this. For her, it is the infantile consciousness and impulses of an individual at the pre-Oedipal stage. She traces evidence of this prelinguistic speech in all its rawness and expressive energy in poetic and avant-garde literary texts, and in the babblings and sounds of her patients, who regress to this stage in their abject state of insanity and emotional distress. It is a vital and creative well of life, which she equates with the maternal, and as such it is a disruptive force. She equates the symbolic order, following Freud and Lacan, with the patriarchal, with the father and the law – the norms of society.

Kristeva arrived from a foreign country. She remains an outsider to France and sympathizes with that which is exiled, marginalized and forgotten. Scene from *Kleiner Mann – ganz groß!* (1938) with Gusti Huber.

Summing up

Postfeminism has moved beyond feminism, acknowledging the difference between the sexes. There is something creative and ethical in this difference, for we define ourselves in relation to the other or the stranger. The feminine stresses the intuitive, the poetic and the body, and some thinkers try to overturn Western metaphysics by stressing the value of the non-rational.

ETHICS AND POLITICS

Philosophers have sought to ground ethics in either society or the rational mind. Ethics either represent a social tradition, which forms us and guides us, or they are written into the fabric of the universe and can be discerned in the individual conscience as a given.

Aristotle suggested that ethics were the product of living in society. The good man was one who contributed his skills and cooperated. Virtues were developed and became a habit. Socrates, however, teased people into questioning the values and laws of the state. These had to be based upon reason, not power plays and prejudice, to be just and true, and therefore worthy of consent. Ethics,

'Man is a political animal.' Life in the Greek *polis* determined social relations and ethical values.

in this tradition, was a more internal, reflective affair, seeking the rational and clearest solution. The conflict between these two positions is called the 'is–ought' debate.

The utilitarians argue that the 'good' is to be worked out in each situation, calculating all the pros and cons. Their maxim is 'the greatest good of the greatest number of people'. Consequences count, not just motives. Ethics are, therefore, determined socially and in situ, although there are general guidelines ('rules'?) that can be applied. But can we always successfully calculate ethics when we are dealing with real people and their feelings?

Immanuel Kant argued that there were moral absolutes – some things were always right and wrong regardless of the situation. He called these categorical imperatives. Thus, stealing is always selfish, and lying is always wrong. But what if a lie can protect an innocent person from the secret police? And who decides what is right?

Postmodernism shuns grand theories and the attempts to ground ethics in fixed 'truths', but it has a real contribution to make. Postmodern philosophers stress how reality is societal and relational; we are not alone.

Contents

No one does wrong knowingly.
SOCRATES

The Genealogy of Morals

Ethical commands and ideas can sometimes be shown to be influenced by society and ideologies of power. Nietzsche traced what he called the genealogy of morals in order to strip them of their absolutist credentials.

In *The Genealogy of Morals*, Nietzsche pursues a historical enquiry into the origin and growth of morality. He traced a fundamental shift back to the Christian era, contrasting this with the classical period. The 'good' was originally linked with the strong and powerful, the nobility. They defined ethics, setting social norms and standards. Courage and bravery, physical prowess and cunning were a priority. The good man was an achiever, one who seized the day and made a difference. He pointed out that, in German, the words for 'bad' and 'poor' were linked by their etymology — *schlecht* and *schlicht*. To be common and plebeian was bad.

The slave ethic

Christianity elevated the plebeian values of the underdog or the slave. An ethics of pity was introduced, with compassion for the poor and weak. This is a cornerstone of Western ethics,

and yet Nietzsche saw this as ultimately embracing an anti-life stance, for it militated against the ego, self-development and awareness. It became a virtue to give of yourself and not to develop yourself. Boldness became arrogance, pride became self-love, and health was spurned for the value of suffering, which

> *The saint, in whom God is well-pleased, is the ideal castrato... Life ends where the 'kingdom of God' begins...*
>
> FRIEDRICH NIETZSCHE,
> *TWILIGHT OF THE IDOLS*

How far have certain forms of Christianity propagated a religion of self-hatred by despising self-fulfilment? The Flagellants of medieval Europe publicly scourged themselves in an attempt to assuage God's wrath for the sins of the population. Woodcut, 1493.

was 'good for the soul'. He castigated the priestly caste in Catholic Christianity for propagating this self-hating system. He also saw repression and self-denial at work in the teaching that rewards came only in heaven. This created an anger, a terrible outrage against

Nietzsche said that the only true Christian who has ever lived died on the cross, and that he would believe Christians if they appeared to be more redeemed. *Crucifixion* by Fra Angelico (c. 1387–1455).

anything that was different and outside the faith. In noble ethics, there was no guilt about giving vent to rage — it was out and could be dealt with. In the slave ethic, anger is repressed.

Basic, animal, human instincts are repressed by reason and *Homo sapiens* (wise man) is distinguished by this drive to elevate one aspect of our being and to ignore the free expression of more

passionate, emotive sides of our natures. This creates an interiorization, which develops into a conscience. We declare war on ourselves thereby!

Nietzsche makes a great deal of sense. Some forms of institutional Christianity have sounded very anti-life, embracing an ascetic ideal that is self-hating and denies the body. The church has not done well at integrating the passions, and has taken the lead from Plato and some Greek thinkers who denigrated the emotions at the expense of reason. This is a far cry from Jesus of Nazareth and his lusty love of life and laughter, embracing the outcast and throwing a party. Even Nietzsche respected the original Jesus: 'There was only one Christian and he died on the cross.' But Nietzsche's attack on the ethics of pity surely goes too far.

The Superman

Ideas of the Superman, of power, elitism and reason, had dire social consequences in the 20th century.

The Superman, or *Übermensch*, was Nietzsche's ideal human being. Supermen developed their skills to the fullest, fulfilled their potential and embraced life – life in the body – with all its verve and passion. They had vision and would move heaven and earth to achieve their goals. Julius Caesar and Napoleon were Supermen; they shook the social order of their day. The Superman concept was lifted by Hitler and twisted out of context. Nietzsche would have deplored his xenophobia and anti-Semitism, as well as the institutionalized savagery of the Nazis. The deeds of the *Übermensch* were meant to liberate and enhance life, not to tread down so many in the pursuit of such a narrow vision.

Napoleon embodied Nietzsche's idea of a Superman. Painting by François Gerard (1770–1837).

Elitism and modernism

The early 20th-century intellectuals, the founders of the modernist project, were disturbingly patrician and elitist. They worked against the backdrop of mass industrialization and mass production, with its corresponding social revolution,

Versions of the golden rule are found in every faith. All ethics has to be grounded in respect for the other. Even postmodernism cannot escape this obligation:

Do to others what you would have them do to you.

JESUS

What you do not wish done to yourself, do not to others.

CONFUCIUS

Let none of you treat your brother in a way he himself would dislike to be treated.

MUHAMMAD

One should seek for others the happiness one desires for oneself.

THE BUDDHA

Modernist intellectuals feared the masses. Lunch break in a Yugoslav factory, 1952 – the first factory in Yugoslavia to have self-administration by the workers.

expanding bourgeoisie and educational programme. The old class divisions were falling down. They shared a hatred and a fear of the masses, disdaining socialist views of universal education as 'dumbing down'. They hated the middle classes with their conformism and rigid views. A social order had to be preserved, an intellectual elite. Aldous Huxley moaned, 'Universal education has created an immense class of what I may call the New Stupid.' T.S. Eliot declared, 'Poets, in our civilization, as it exists at present, must be difficult.' The literature and art of modernism contained a declaration of separateness. Was this not another form of the noble versus the plebeian?

Consequences

Self-hatred is one thing, but the desire to aid and give to another is not purely negative, as Nietzsche believed. It can, indeed, enhance one's own self-worth in the process, expressing solidarity. The attitude is summed up in the golden rule found in all faiths: 'Do unto others as you would have them do unto you.' Nietzsche's views were dangerous when he characterized altruistic efforts as misspent energy, supporting a weaker form of life that deserved to be ignored. He might not have foreseen the consequences of this attitude, but the early 20th century embraced an unhealthy interest in eugenics, the desire to rid the human race of genetic defects. Early socialists were not innocent of this, seeing a way towards utopia, and Hitler applied a ruthless form in his attempt to create the master race. The myth of racial purity, and the aim of genetic perfection are a potent cocktail when mixed.

Postmodern Ethics?

Can ethics be possible in postmodern thinking where all fixed points and authorities are questioned? What sorts of politics are possible, beyond anarchism or quietism and disinterest?

For the postmodernists, all is interpretation, mediated through our conceptual, human senses. Reality in the raw, truth in its purity, cannot be present to us. Such is the human or postmodern condition. This can often be understood as a dethronement of meaning itself that produces an utter relativism.

Scruton's criticisms

The English philosopher Roger Scruton, Professor of Philosophy at Boston University, in his text of 1994, *Modern Philosophy, An Introduction and Survey*, castigates Derrida and others, fearing moral relativism:

By demonstrating that all law and interdiction, all meaning and value, all that troubles, contains or limits us is our own invention, the devil fosters the belief that everything is permitted... then the temptation of the liberator is irresistible. 'Ruin the sacred truths,' as Marvel said; pull down the order that surrounds you; not only do you affirm yourself against it, you also liberate your fellows...

By the 'devil' he means the forces of deceit and destruction, 'the father of lies'. He goes on to attack deconstruction as irresponsible:

Texts do not have a single authoritative meaning; there is a 'free play of meaning' and anything goes. In short, we are liberated from meaning...

Scruton's attack perhaps reveals the bias of the Anglo-

Saxon, analytical philosophical tradition against that of the continent. He goes too far and seriously misunderstands Derrida, at least. Derrida has never stood for a total overthrow of reason or meaning. It is a question of balance, and

ideology of the day, as well as our own experience in reading and reacting to a text, all come into play. Just what is it that we are reading? Let us be aware, Derrida tells us. He does not destroy meaning. If anything, he liberates it from any one agenda

> *What is called 'deconstruction'...*
> *has never, never opposed*
> *institutions as such, philosophy as*
> *such, discipline as such... Because,*
> *however affirmative deconstruction*
> *is, it is affirmative in a way that*
> *is not simply positive, not simply*
> *conservative, not simply a way of*
> *repeating the given institution. I*
> *think that the life of an institution*
> *implies that we are able to*
> *criticize, to transform, to open the*
> *institution to its own future...*
>
> JACQUES DERRIDA,
> ROUNDTABLE DISCUSSION
> AT VILLANOVA UNIVERSITY
> IN 1994

Does postmodernism place us in the 'land of do-as-you-please', where all values are relative?

of recognizing a place for the emotive and that which cannot easily be expressed.

Derrida does not teach that a text can have any number of meanings ad infinitum as we desire. A text can be read in different ways, true, but there is only a finite number of interpretations possible. The conscious intention of the author, the unconscious influences, social concerns and

or ideology. He is saying, 'Let us see what can be found in a text.'

Derrida has stated that his deconstructive method is an act of love, teasing out honest truth and recognizing different positions. Why should we believe just what we are told to, or do as we are told? Let us be aware and see clearly.

Power and Prejudice

Postmodernists challenge us to see the influences of society and power in our view of reality. 'Knowledge' and ethics are not unconditioned by our surroundings.

The negative and ironical questioning of the postmodern is necessary to be true to oneself. Unconscious and social, economic and political influences, and the received corpus of wisdom and tradition that is handed down to us all affect us. Foucault, for example, dug deep as a literary and social archaeologist to demonstrate the power plays he saw at work in so many of our systems – our ideas of sexuality, attitudes to madness, crime and punishment – regulate and exclude. His method of social archaeology used the term '*épistème*' at first. *Épistème* was the undergirding system of thought and controlling concepts in each age. The Renaissance, for example, saw similitudes everywhere, links between things and words, such as the 'theatre of life'. The Enlightenment broke these links apart, classifying differences and seeking rational and mathematical representations. The 'modern' age used history as its *épistème*, understanding human life in terms of

economics, biology and psychology: hence Marxism.

Living in discourses

In his later works, Foucault prefers to speak of discourses rather than *épistèmes*. A social discourse is a view of things,

Two hippies respond to the policeman directing them away from 10 Downing Street with flowers. This is a subversive action, robbing certain symbols of their power by juxtaposing opposing ones.

FOUCAULT'S CASES

Foucault became involved in specific and local struggles, such as gay rights, and championed the release of a petty thief in 1980 (who later reoffended and embarrassed Foucault). He admitted that he had made an error in supporting the establishment of an Islamic government in Iran. He thought that their sense of religious duty would safeguard personal liberty.

Before the end of the 18th century, man did not exist. As the archaeology of our thought easily shows, man is an invention of a recent date. And perhaps one nearing its end.

MICHEL FOUCAULT, *THE ORDER OF THINGS*

taking in many ideologies and disciplines. When we speak of 'human nature', which *épistème* or discourse are we working with?

Foucault spoke of the 'end of man'. His 'end' was partly that of the Cartesian self, the rational, defined mind, cool, separate from body and world. We are now seen as much more a part of the body, the environment, the social network in which we are reared. He also meant that all talk of 'human nature' can only be in discourse and not in any pure knowledge from a privileged position outside discourse. We live in discourse like fish in water.

Not very constructive?

Critics would say thinkers such as Foucault have very little to say that is constructive. Foucault sought a radical philosophy that acted as a counterculture to power structures. He exposes the problem, but does not seem to address it. 'Free people to seek pleasure' seems to have been his motto. This easily becomes implosive and selfish. When we are freed from received traditions, where do we find value?

Postmodern Care

Many postmodern thinkers are politically active and embrace ethical causes. This appears to give the lie to the charge of moral relativism commonly made against postmodernism.

Derrida is concerned with issues of peace and justice, and has spoken of deconstruction as an act of hospitality, in the sense of making 'the other' welcome – the other point of view, the other interpretation. Justice is a category that refuses ultimate deconstruction – there might be different ideas of what is just, but the 'just' just is. Justice

THE OTHER

A key epistemological idea in postmodernism is the role of alterity: the other. Thus, postmodernism has an inbuilt ethical dimension. This entered philosophy through the work of Emmanuel Levinas, a Lithuanian Jew (another émigré) who introduced the work of Husserl and Heidegger to France in the 1930s. This account of experience and being was fundamentally altered by the introduction of the other. Levinas drew upon his Judaic lore and the ethics of the Torah that told people to love their neighbour as themselves. The story of the patriarch Jacob relates an episode in which he is reconciled with his brother Esau: 'For to see your face is like seeing the face of God…' (Genesis 33:10).

The relationship with, and the existence of, the other puts us under question. We cannot hold a closed-up analysis and dialogue with our solitary self; we are relational beings, and in that relationship, we define our being. The obligations of one to another are fundamental and precede any idea of contracts that we might seek to establish. I cannot just have it my way when someone else is involved. This is a hint of Derrida's justice that 'just is'. Being is not just 'me' and my awareness, perceptions and experiences. This was a different current of thought from the existentialism of Sartre, who sought freedom for the self.

> *There is, in the face, the supreme*
> *authority that commands, and I*
> *always say it is the word of God.*
> *There is the word of God in the*
> *other, a non-thematized word.*
>
> EMMANUEL LEVINAS,
> *THE PROXIMITY OF THE OTHER*

Levinas drew upon the ethics of the Torah, the Law of Moses.

demands our human rights. Internationalism and racial harmony are close to Derrida's heart. Derrida, like some other thinkers, is seeing life as an immigrant to France. He was born and raised in Algeria, coming to Paris in 1949.

Julia Kristeva, another émigré, is active with the French anti-racism group, SOS Racisme. She works with the mentally disturbed as an analyst, revealing a caring and compassionate side in her writings about melancholy, depression and the mind. She seeks tolerance and inclusion and their wholeness and healing.

Luce Irigaray has written about the ethics of sexual difference, moving beyond male/female battles for ascendancy and power. It is in their difference and their meeting that true liberation lies, and not in doing violence to human nature by seeking an artificial androgyny. She promotes adequate health care, and challenges media-controlled ideas of beauty. Tolerance is a watchword of gender difference, infirmities, looks and age.

> *We must either transcend the Other*
> *or allow oneself to be transcended*
> *by him. The essence of relationships*
> *between consciousness… is conflict.*
>
> JEAN-PAUL SARTRE,
> *BEING AND NOTHINGNESS*

Open to the Other

Justice and peace issues are partly grounded in the universal, human experience of alterity – otherness – and partly in the possibility of the future with its hopes and fresh beginnings.

Ethical philosophers have always debated the make-up of the true ground of ethics. Social and individual approaches both tend to seek an external set of values, a code, a way of things that can justify their position – nature, religion, conscience or whatever. They seek something spoken from the heavens or written in human nature.

There is no society without faith, without trust in the other.

JACQUES DERRIDA

THE UNIVERSALITY TEST

Even Kant's categorical imperatives – absolute rules of right and wrong – were determined by his universality test. You imagined what would happen if you acted in a certain way, for example stealing. Would rights be respected and social life possible?

The question 'Are there such things as moral facts?' is hotly debated. Even if morality is seen as part of human discourse, then there are terms and concepts that can have validity even if they are not objective, external things totally outside our social

The future always gives birth to hope. Things can change, as with the collapse of the Berlin Wall in November 1989.

As soon as you address the other, as soon as you are open to the future, as soon as you have a temporal experience of waiting for the future, of waiting for someone to come: that is the opening of experience. Someone is to come, is now to come. Justice and peace will have to do with this coming of the other, with the promise...

JACQUES DERRIDA

lives. This overrides the old 'is–ought' debate and presents useful, value-laden concepts that we cannot do without to live our lives, such as 'freedom' or 'justice'. Does money exist, for example? It is a human creation, but we feel it if we do not have any! Terms such as 'torture' have a factual and an ethical content.

At root, though, all can agree on ethics as a form of social contract whereby we agree to respect certain rights so that people can live in society.

111

The End of History?

Postmodernists can speak of teleology (the point or purpose of something) and eschatology (the last things) in a sociological sense – the 'end of history' and 'the end of man'.

The American historian Francis Fukuyama published *The End of History and the Last Man* in 1992. In this best-selling work, he proclaims the triumph of capitalism at the close of the second millennium. Western, liberal democracy is changing the world for the better. Its values are spreading; the Soviet Bloc has collapsed and is embracing the free-market economy. Just as Hegel postulated an emerging liberal society and Marx one of equal opportunity, capitalism has produced the results. Thus, we are dealing with 'the end of history', the most perfect form of society and government imaginable. The 'Last Man' stands at the end of this process, and waves goodbye to all earlier forms of social organization. All dictatorships must crumble and give way to this rising tide, like King Canute retreating before the incoming waves. Post-capitalist, democratic humanity is at the end of human social development.

This is good news, gospel, evangel.

Not quite an end?

It may be true that Fukuyama's vision is to be preferred to Iran under the ayatollahs, with its fatwas and stifling of dissent, or Saddam Hussein's dicatorship in Iraq, for example, but is it really the most perfect form of society? Derrida has presented a biting critique of Fukuyama in *Spectres of Marx*. He points out that much of the world is rejecting Western free-market democracy, such as sections of the Islamic world, and that capitalism has its own power structures and agendas. It is not

> It is possible that if events continue to unfold as they have done over the past few decades, the idea of a universal and directional history leading up to liberal democracy may become more plausible to people, and that the relativist impasse of modern thought will in a sense solve itself.
>
> FRANCIS FUKUYAMA,
> THE END OF HISTORY AND THE LAST MAN

Fukuyama's ideal of the triumph of capitalism and the end of dictatorships is not shared by everyone. Here, Iranians hold up images of their ayatollah.

as pure as the driven snow. How much are values formed by big business? Derrida warns, 'never in history has the horizon of the thing whose survival is being celebrated been as dark, threatening and threatened'.

Baudrillard saw capitalism as turning people into things, as consumers with products, as did another French thinker, Herbert Marcuse (1898–1979), who described capitalist humanity as one-dimensional, isolated consumers with false needs. This is hardly the blueprint for utopia.

Fukuyama admits that the

> *... never have violence, inequality, exclusion, famine, and thus economic oppression affected as many human beings in the history of the Earth and of humanity...*
>
> JACQUES DERRIDA,
> *SPECTRES OF MARX*

actual practice of liberal democracy can be far from perfect, but the ideal cannot be improved upon. Others respond that this is a virtual reality, not an actual reality.

113

Spectres

Derrida's 'spectres' suggest the abiding power of ideas that society has tried to consign to the rubbish bin of history. They are dead, but they will not lie down, outmoded ideas that are still full of insights. They haunt us, though we try to ignore them.

Derrida makes great play of spectres, or his concept of *spectralité*. He opens *Spectres of Marx* with the first line of *The Communist Manifesto*: 'A spectre is haunting Europe, the spectre of communism.' He then turns to Hamlet's ghost and the role of the spectre in looking backwards and forwards. The ghost makes us face up to what has taken place, and where we should be going. In Shakespeare's play,

THE DEVELOPING WORLD

It is tempting to think that the postmodern condition is a symptom of the West's developed capitalism, born of a luxury of opinions and economic security. People who are struggling for freedom or to survive are not so self-indulgent. The answer is not so simple. There are groups who resist the postmodern as another Western import. Others assert local, national and traditional languages and customs over against the postmodern sense of ironical mishmash. Yet others embrace postmodernism in culture or in ideology. Ethnic music can be mixed with new technology and rock beats, borrowed and swapped and sampled across regions. Indian cinema and Thai fiction are open to postmodern influences. The South-East Asian economy has embraced the idea of the simulacrum – the virtual-reality sign – trading fake designer clothes, watches and CDs, which, in some cases, are just as good as the originals. Spot the difference.

The postmodern use of *différance* (being aware of the fluidity of meaning) and *aporia* (lacunas and hidden agendas in texts) can be appropriated by the developing world to protest about marginalization. Human discourse includes more than the Eurocentric, and the existence of groups of nations opposed to Western liberalism, such as the Islamic world, is a form of textual slippage. There are other interpretations, and that which has not been said. Some movements and parties in the developing world are utilizing this dimension, and embracing a postmodernism of the left, such as the Sandanistas in Nicaragua.

Hamlet sees his father's ghost on the battlements of Elsinore Castle. Illustration by Robert Dudley (fl. 1858–93).

the ghost's face is covered by a visor until Hamlet is ready to listen. Then we see, face to face.

While Marxism as a system might be defunct, and we cannot glibly embrace it again in a doctrinaire fashion, it has abiding insights and values that we neglect at our peril. It is based upon the prophetic tradition in the Hebrew scriptures, which speaks of peace and justice. We need a counterculture to expose the weaknesses and moral failings of capitalism. Marxism is dead, but it will not lie down.

Derrida's idea of messianicity comes into focus here. He uses it in a general, secular sense for the future, which must always be open. Hope must always be possible. When we declare that the end

has come, there can be no more to hope for or to grow for. The show must go on.

> **Summing up**
>
> Postmodernists defer the niceties of ethical theory, avoiding metanarratives and grand theories. They embrace the local and the particular, affirming the necessity of respecting human rights as things that are self-evident and given. The existence of alterity shows this, as does any hope of forming society. There is no appeal to any external rules; values are discerned within the discourse, in the relationship with the other.
>
> Postmodern approaches to politics stress how we can never have a perfect system, we can never reach an end; we live with the incomplete and constantly strive to improve, seeking justice for the other.

THE EDGE OF REALITY

Early 20th-century philosophy tended to be dominated by logical analysis, which precluded any meaningful speech about transcendence and the spiritual. The philosopher Bertrand Russell (1872–1970) championed logical atomism, whereby sentences were stripped down to their logical component parts. The Vienna Circle, or the logical positivists, worked along similar lines, arguing that philosophy was really a subdivision of empirical science. It was a useful tool to analyse concepts and to clarify. All talk of metaphysics was stuff and nonsense. A thing only had meaning if it was empirically testable.

Ludwig Wittgenstein came from a

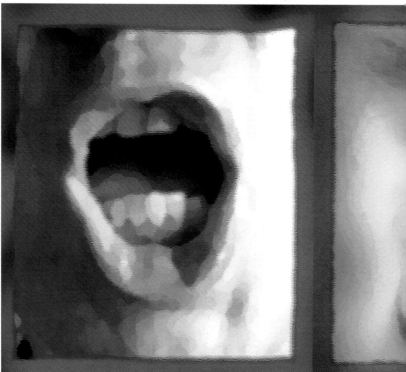

To hear inexpressible things?

Viennese family to work with Russell at Cambridge in 1911. His early views were those of logical atomism, and he produced his first major philosophical work in 1922, the *Tractatus Logico-Philosophicus*. The text begins with the claim: 'The world is all that is the case.'

In Wittgenstein's later works, particularly *Philosophical Investigations* (1953), he abandoned the logical positivism of his youth. He saw philosophy's error in seeking meaning beyond the use of language. Meaning is to be found in the use of language, and there are different 'language games', each obeying different conceptual rules. Artistic or emotive discourse was different from scientific, rational discourse. It was not 'nonsense' for being different.

What can words mean, and is what we cannot speak of unreal? Wittgenstein opened up views of language that were seedbeds for the postmodern thinkers that followed. Derrida and others have courted the expressive, the imaginative and even the mystical. The empirical is just one 'slice of the cake'.

Contents

Of what we cannot speak we must remain silent.

LUDWIG WITTGENSTEIN,
TRACTATUS LOGICO-PHILOSOPHICUS

Stretching Language

Postmodern thinkers have helped to stretch language to its limits, and have tried to make room for the non-rational in discourse.

Deconstruction, undecidability and the rejection of the logic of binary opposites have opened up the world of discourse in a deeper and richer sense. The poetic and the imaginative have their vital part to play. The 'linguistic turn', whereby meaning is found within discourse and not beyond it, is very much a feature of the postmodern, but, perhaps, new ways have been opened up to allow forms of discourse regarded as suspect by rationalist thinkers.

This spread sums up some key concepts in postmodern thought, which outline the new directions and possibilities in philosophical thinking.

Chora

This Greek word for 'space' or 'place' is used to signify the hidden depths of human personality or 'the soul'. This is the preverbal self, the state of being of the newborn infant. Kristeva calls this time the semiotic, the time when we 'speak' in signs, gestures and grunts, and experience colours,

sounds and sensations without the language to order and 'name' them. The body and its sensitivity to touch are primary.

Jouissance

This term, taken from the English literary heritage (as in Spenser's *Faerie Queene*), was coined by Lacan. He saw this as any experience – psychological and physical – that the human organism found too much to bear. It was 'deep feelings' territory. He tended to see this in a negative light, as a silent force that blocked psychological change and frustrated the therapist – the compulsion for a client to repeat the same mistakes. It was a form of suffering that the psyche craved. This sounds rather unattractive, and various thinkers have dusted this off to stress the 'enjoyment/joy' meaning. *Jouissance* is rapture and bliss, the extreme emotions felt in the presence of the beloved, a striking sunrise, a baby's smile, religious or artistic experience. It is the depths, and the extremities of language and human communication.

The other
The concept of 'the other' includes space, a space between subject and object, or person and person. In postmodernism, space is not empty but creative. According to Baudrillard in *Fatal Strategies*, 'The Other is what stops me from constantly repeating myself.'

The void
The void is a term derived from Eastern thought, particularly Buddhist philosophy. It was taken up by Heidegger's existential philosophy as a symbol for being. It is a teaser. What do we mean by it? The void can be nothing, space, the hole that allows other things to be, the blank that acts as a stage. For Heidegger, 'being' was light, fluid, empty and a sort of nothing that allowed everything to be. Postmodernists use this idea to remind us that reason is not the only way of seeing the world. There is that which defies analysis and comprehension. Kristeva has claimed that rational discourse 'is only one more interpretation which cannot see that it embraces a void'.

Babies lack the ability to express in words what they experience in the world around them. Instead, they respond with gurgles and movements. Study of this 'language' of signs is called semiotics, from the Greek word meaning 'of signs'.

The Gift

'The gift' is a key term in postmodernism. It deals with questions of the givenness of existence and gratitude. It opens up questions of social order, possibility and impossibility, and revisits the hoary questions of presence and absence.

Speaking of the gift – the gift of life and being – carries us into the interplay of absence and presence. Something is given; we receive it and live in it. Yet nothing can ever be really and completely given, for the metaphysics of presence must be questioned. Nothing is totally present to us, in the raw. All is filtered through interpretation and is now *and* not yet. Derrida makes great play of this, and fears any idea of total gift and presence as though that is it and it is over. He works with constant horizons of possibility, always wishing the future to remain open. The gift must always be now and not yet, partly ahead of us.

He says that he dreams of the impossible, not the narrowly defined possible. Kant saw the rational, enlightened person as being adult; they confined themselves to only what was possible. Derrida dares to dream of something *tout autre*, totally other. He

Expect the unexpected. Be amazed and go beyond your concepts. *Sunrise* by Giuseppe Pellizza (1868–1907).

speaks of *l'invention de l'autre*, 'the incoming of the other', that shatters the horizons of the possible and allows us to drive where we cannot go. Expect the unexpected. Berlin Walls do come tumbling down. Derrida thus links the concept of the gift with hospitality and justice – impossibilities that might be. Black South Africa could be free!

Is the gift possible?

Derrida reminds us that when a donor gives a gift, then the recipient is indebted to the giver. Also, the giver gains honour and prestige. This is a troublesome dichotomy, an *aporia* of giving. The donor may intend to give freely and graciously, but the social dynamic is still set in motion. *Aporias* are not barriers for Derrida, but signs that the impossible can be dreamed and we can move beyond. Despite the social obligations of the gift, we have to boldly ignore this and receive and be. We have to give without giving up, behaving almost madly in order to believe that this is possible. Might not the dynamics and contradictions of religions (for example, law and grace) stem from this *aporia* of the gift? God gives freely, but demands and status are thus created.

The gift and God

Speaking of the gift immediately opens up religious questions and feelings. The gift of life, or the world, and relationships, and the whole dynamic of redemption in Christianity revolve around a freely given gift. Derrida toys with religious concepts. He has said that deconstruction is structured like a religion, like a prayer for the wholly other, for justice and peace. He seeks to deconstruct totalities, or systems of religion that codify and prescribe. These have been called false idolatries (for example, Aaron's golden calf rather than the Unseen God of Moses: Exodus 32:1–8). Theologians and philosophers debate whether speech about God moves into new realms, evoking something that is and is not, the now and the not yet. Something meets us (a visitation, or partially so) that surprises, leaving us rubbing our eyes in wonder.

The Big Story?

Postmodernism is sceptical of talking about metanarratives – grand narratives, 'big stories' about life, the universe and everything.

Metanarratives are stories that reach beyond the limits of knowledge and reason. The principle of deconstruction gets to work as we see the cultural influences and limitations in any grand narrative that has ever been told. We are now aware that we are influenced by the age we live in, and so we do not believe that there can be any pure truth that spans the ages. This does not only mean the belief systems of the world religions, but scientific and secular metanarratives too. Marxism, for example, was a belief system that predicted a worldwide uprising of workers and a final age of equality and freedom. This was seen as inevitable progress. Science works within a narrative dubbed the grand march, whereby we are always moving upwards and progressing in knowledge and efficiency.

The French thinker Jean-François Lyotard argued that the age of metanarratives was over. We must embrace lots of little, local concerns now, and stop trying to connect them up in false, humanly created systems.

Technology is therefore a game pertaining not to the true, the just, or the beautiful, etc., but to efficiency…

JEAN-FRANÇOIS LYOTARD, *THE POSTMODERN CONDITION*

Reason and the absolute

The philosopher Hegel taught another metanarrative. He believed that human reason was capable of a 'theory of everything', the more we knew and discovered. As reason gradually overcame the taboo and the irrational, things would become clearer. He saw reason, or mind, as emerging Spirit, and thought of the 'whole' as the absolute or God. There was something objective out there that we could fully comprehend one day. This theory now lies in tatters as postmodernism avoids talk of the absolute, and scorns our ability ever to grasp the whole of reality. Words and concepts simply fail us.

Science is not solid any more!

Science is not the pure, totally objective truth that it has made itself out to be, and empirical observation might be able to probe and perceive only one dimension of reality. As particle physics tells us, nothing is actually solid. Everything is energy that moves. We, and each speck of dust, are dancing collections of clusters of energy. The more we analyse things, the less physical matter becomes and the normal rules are left behind. Dare we say it seems to be more spiritual?

We know in part…

We need more awe, reverence and humility to admit we do not, and probably cannot, know, understand or explain some things in life. It is rather like Van Gogh's painting of a peasant's shoes, *A Pair of Shoes*. A consumer/analytical model sees a pair of old boots, and sees their value in their utility only. Yet, as a work of art, Van Gogh was saying something about the lot of the worker who wore them. They speak of his concerns and struggles. There is that extra quality of the personal and emotive. Ironically, the art world slaps a 'value' on paintings such as this, and they are trapped in the consumer system.

A Pair of Shoes by Vincent Van Gogh (1853–90).

123

What Will We Become?

Are metanarratives possible when technology and human life change so rapidly? How might we evolve and what new possibilities will be set before us?

Lyotard took the debate about metanarratives in a new direction when he argued that the future and our knowledge are completely unpredictable. The rise of information technology could develop all kinds of super-possibilities, and humans might leave the body behind altogether, utilizing machines. He was filled with fears about this, warning about the increasing emergence of the inhuman as technology grew and grew. It is a scenario that has to be imagined, and these fears take shape in some science fiction, such as the novels of William Gibson or popular movies like *The Terminator*. In these, it is hard to see where man and machine starts and finishes. Lyotard argued that we are so dependent upon computers and technology that we are already cyborgs.

In one of Lyotard's modern fables, he plays with the idea that future generations might develop to such a stage of mental life, separate from matter, that they can escape the

THE HERO

In *Postmodern Fables*, Lyotard called his advanced life form 'the hero', and its escape is its 'exile' from the dying universe:

The human species is not the hero of the fable. It is a complex form of organizing energy... the exile's hero... will have to be more complex than the human species is at the time when the fable is being recounted, since this species does not have the means of its exile, although it is the most complex organization of energy we know in the universe... That's why the fable lets it be understood that the exile's hero, destined to survive the destruction of terrestrial life, will not be a mere survivor, since it will not be alive in the sense we understand the word...

Perhaps it would resemble the alien intelligence that communicates through the monoliths in Arthur C. Clarke's *2001: A Space Odyssey*? We cannot know. Any 'big story' told today is flawed and incomplete. What will come to be? How will things change?

Nuremburg Rally, Germany, September 1935. Such triumphalism as this can deny rights to those who have different views.

entropy of the universe (the final run down or burnout of all matter and energy). What would human life have become by that point?

Dogmatism

Metanarratives are rejected because they are impossible or incomplete. They also tend to be rigid and dogmatic, and have often used terror and force to keep themselves in power. Think of Christianity's legacy with the Inquisition and burnings at the stake, or fundamentalist Islam with its beheadings and amputations. Secular ideologies can have Gulags and firing squads too. Even materialistic views of science can be mocking and

dismissive to people with spiritual beliefs in a so-called enlightened age. When we think we are totally and wholly right, and the other is totally wrong, then anger and impatience abound, and intolerance can wipe out any sense of human rights in extreme cases. Derrida argues that logocentrism is based upon a violent act, the marking of clay or paper with writing tools. Its view of things is imposed.

Perhaps there is a tentative way back for metanarratives, but not in the form in which we have known them.

125

How Big Can Our Vision Be?

Perhaps we cannot codify, analyse and define reality in totality. Our ideas are always provisional and time-conditioned, but might they not hint at or grasp something of the nature and mystery of life?

Can we say nothing at all apart from lots of little, local stories, as Lyotard asserts? There might be no stepping outside human language, beyond the text, but within it there are all kinds of meanings and hints of meanings. We live and move within language, and our experience of reality comes to us through that. It is all a package deal.

> *God is spirit, and his worshippers must worship in spirit and in truth.*
>
> JESUS, JOHN 4:24

Hints of the beyond?

What hints of reality and beyond might come through the text of our language?

Derrida has stressed that deconstruction is an act of love and should not be negative and cynical. It is purgative, open and honest, seeking truth and exposing shaky foundations. It seeks to lay out what we can and cannot say, what has been influenced

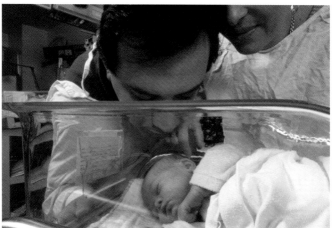

Life is a gift that we did not plan or ask for. Is this just by blind chance, or some deeper design?

by a particular culture and so on.

Some postmodern philosophers are suggestively open to the notion of spirit, transcendence or God. They use the word 'God', but are rather ambiguous about what actual content they give this. As a rich symbol, it suggests the new, the beyond, the open and the mysterious. There is a general desire to 'turn' or to 'return' to ideas, symbols and values from a pre-modern age, but not in an uncritical fashion.

GOD?

When discussing belief in God, we always have to investigate what people mean by 'God'. For many in the Western world, this means a childish and mythological idea of an old man in the sky with beard and white robe. The history of religions reveals much more awe-inspiring notions than this. The biblical view of God can be anthropomorphic, using human imagery for God, but it is also sublime and spiritual. God is spirit, undefinable, beyond us. When Moses knelt before the

Life flows; it is not static with fixed points.

burning bush and asked what God's name was, the reply came 'I am'. No name, no form, just being. Modern theologians such as Paul Tillich have spoken of God as 'Ultimate Concern' or 'the Ground of our Being'. No beard, just being.

What all postmodernists would reject is God as the foundation, the sure, fixed point upon which the whole of metaphysics and all knowledge is built. There are no foundations or fixed points. Life flows. But is their 'God' any more than a symbol of moral and spiritual values? The radical Cambridge theologian Don Cupitt takes this line. One of his key ideas is that, as we cannot step outside language, all traditional concepts of God as the beyond are meaningless. God is just the sum total of our values. If we cannot escape language, can God be real outside our minds?

God and the Postmodernists

How do postmodern philosophers use the idea of 'God'? What does this mean for them – is it just rich imagery, or is there a suggestion of profound depths to reality?

Kristeva uses neo-Freudian language about the Imaginary Father (for Freud, God was an 'ideal', an illusion, based upon the earthly father's authority and internalized as moral conscience. As Freud put it, 'At bottom, God is nothing more than an exalted father'). She is enchanted and fascinated by these 'illusions', though. She argues that we need the old illusions, and she talks of God as a projection, though a necessary one. In her writing on the creed, the central statement of Christian belief, she declares that she is not a believer, but she unveils the psychological dynamics in Christian beliefs. She sees these as code for inner ideals and transformations that are very real within us, but not 'out there'. Kristeva, working as an analyst, sees the worth of this: 'The result is not to prepare that other for some sort of transcendental existence, but rather to open up as yet undefined possibilities in this world' (*In the Beginning was Love*).

Love is...
It has been pointed out that Kristeva might hint at real transcendence when she speaks of love, for this comes to us and draws us out, it acts between the lover and the beloved, or the parent and the child. It seems to be more than human, and does not arise within us. She likes medieval definitions of a person as one who can be affected by the love of another, using the dictum of

Is a god what we need, then? A god who can upset the limits of the possible, melt the ancient glaciers, a god who can make a future for us. A god carries on the breath of the cosmos, the song of the poets, the respiration of lovers... not waiting passively for the god to come, but by conjuring him up among us, within us, as resurrection and transfiguration of blood, of flesh through a language and an ethics that is ours.

LUCE IRIGARAY,
AN ETHICS OF SEXUAL DIFFERENCE

Bernard of Clairvaux, *'Ego affectus est'* ('I am one who feels or is affected by another'). The Enlightenment brought the idea of a person as a solitary, thinking subject. The space in which love occurs sounds almost as though it is beyond space/time and this is most curious.

What might God really be, what potential does the word hold? *Ancient of Days* by William Blake (1757–1827).

Ancient and yet to come

Luce Irigaray wants to believe in a God who has feminine characteristics, 'archi-ancient and forever future'. She seeks the 'birth' of a new God, who is not yet formed, and rejects the old, patriarchal father as a foundation for the whole Western metaphysical system. This God provided eternal authentication for a whole system of thought and hierarchy. But there is room for God differently envisaged, always ahead of us, moving, alive and not static. God is a form of the other, drawing us out, meeting us, creating space to be. She harks back to the idea of woman as other, as stranger and dark continent, mysterious hole, and asks, 'What riches can come forth from this?' There the new birthing of God will be located.

In the Air

Playful, poetic philosophy overturns traditional metaphysics, but moves closer to the sacred scriptures, ironically. Fluid images fit the God of the Bible much better than foundations and fixed points.

Irigaray plays with the four elements of air, earth, fire and water, seeing classical philosophy and metaphysics (all ideas about foundations and God) being built upon the earth. It is the other three elements that are more suited to the language of mystery and mysticism. 'The metaphysical is written neither on/in water, nor on/in air, neither on/in fire. Its ek-sistance is founded on the solid,' says Irigaray in *The Forgetting of Air*. Ironically, the God of the Bible is often symbolized by just these fluid elements – blazing fire, rushing wind and springs of 'living' water.

Touch

In *An Ethics of Sexual Difference*, Irigaray stresses that the body is prior to language, as the primary means of communication: 'Before orality comes to be, touch is already in existence. No nourishment can compensate for the grace or work of touching… The most subtly necessary guardian of my life is the other's flesh. Approaching and speaking to me with his hands…' The physical is where it all starts. As one recent commentator on her work put it: 'Text is also tissue.'

The open air

Sensuality is not inferior to reason and language. It is all a part of a whole. Words have to be earthed to be lived. They have to be part of the breath of life. Irigaray makes much of the air we breathe as a symbol of life and the space that surrounds us, the space that gives us 'room to breathe', to be ourselves and to relate to the other. Air fills our lungs at birth. We live in it from then on. Air = space around us = an opening.

Biblical metaphors for God use fluid, often intangible terms such as the air or wind, or water, or fire.

… the most intimate perception of the flesh escapes… every assimilation into discourse… Scent or premonition between my very self and the other, this memory of the flesh as the place of approach means ethical fidelity to incarnation. To destroy it is to risk the suppression of alterity, both the God's and the other's. Thereby dissolving any possibility of access to transcendence.

LUCE IRIGARAY,
AN ETHICS OF SEXUAL DIFFERENCE

Touch is communication beyond words. *The Creation of Adam* by Michelangelo Buonarroti (1475–1564).

Irigaray discusses her idea of an opening, a clearing, in all systems, discourse and analysis of phenomena. This opening allows for mystery, transcendence, freedom and the unpredictable. She plays with the idea of the opening as an O, a hole, and a circle, the whole. There is a hole in the Whole that we cannot grasp with our words and concepts. It eludes us.

Body Language

Postmodern feminist thinkers focus on the body and the value of touch and sensual communication. The mystery called God is also the mystery of our deepest self, a spirit enveloped in flesh.

In *Equal to Whom?* Irigaray plays with the conventional Christian terminology of 'incarnation' meaning 'in a body'. The incarnation, for Christian theology, is the unique presence of God in Christ; Irigaray uses incarnation for all of us – 'the incarnation of all bodies (men's and women's) as potentially divine'. Our personalities live 'in a body'. We are embodied beings, or enveloped in flesh, as she puts it. She sees the physical body, with its skin surfaces, nerve endings and caresses, as the primary vehicle of communication besides language and abstract ideas. If God is to be anything to us, it must be on

Jesus heals the leper. Late 12th-century manuscript illumination from *The Four Gospels*, Mount Athos Monastery, Iberon, Greece.

this level, through touch, and flesh-and-blood reality:

Every stage in the life of Christ is noted and described in the Gospels as an event of the body: conception, birth, growth, fasting in the desert, immersion in the River Jordan, treks to the mountain or walks along the water's edge, meals, festivals, the laying-on of hands, the draining of physical strength after a healing, transfiguration, trials, suffering, death, resurrection, ascension… His life cannot be reduced to speeches given in closed, airless structures, or to repetitive rituals and disincarnation… It cannot be reduced to moral injunctions or to debates among clerics…

> The face of 'God' is the unveiling, the staggering vision of the construction we are, the tiny and great lies… An unveiling that happens by surprise, by accident, and with a brutality that shatters…
>
> HÉLÈNE CIXOUS,
> *THREE STEPS ON THE LADDER OF WRITING*

Secrets and bliss

For Hélène Cixous, words can stretch, reach out, play and

express magical things. She uses terms such as 'mystery', 'enigma', 'unknown' and 'inexplicable' frequently. She writes, 'the soul is the magic of attention', and she finds bliss and surprise in aesthetic encounters — music, art or a literary text. Something of this surprise is found in the space between self and the other, this mysterious emptiness that lets be. Here is an epiphany, an encounter of love.

She speaks of her 'secret': 'At the heart of it lies a soft gleaming pearl like the flash of eternity at the heart of a moment...'

She draws upon the works of medieval mystics and sums up her vision — that of the other, the free space, the bliss, the mystery — as 'looking straight at God'.

This imaginative, creative thinker leaves us with an ambiguity about the exact nature of her 'God', like some of the other writers mentioned. On one level, her 'God' is the deepest level of her being, what Jung would call the Self in relation to the self. Yet there is a hint of transcendence, for when we journey so deep down, we go beyond. Do we hit God at the deepest layer of our being?

Why is the pearl in the shell such a rich metaphor for the self or soul in mystical texts?

Deconstruction and God

Jacques Derrida often touches on religious themes and enjoys debating with theologians. Religion is a vast sea of signifiers that say something worthwhile.

Derrida verges on the theological at times, speaking of giving and the search for 'Whom do we give to?' What is a valid response to the gift? He has written movingly about the phrase *mysterium tremendum et fascinans* – the 'tremendous and fascinating mystery' that makes us tremble at the heart of life. He encourages theologians to discuss his views and seems to respect

GOD IS…

The meaning of God for Derrida has been described by one commentator, John D. Caputo in *Deconstruction in a Nutshell*, as:

'something unforseeable, unforegraspable, something to come… something nameless'. This is 'the Other', as well as the demands of neighbour. Derrida's views can be summed up as saying that 'God' goes by other names 'like justice, hospitality, testimony, the gift – and democracy. For God is the name of the other, any other, no matter whom.'

those who have faith. He claims, 'I quite rightly pass for an atheist' but it is not clear exactly what he means by this. He speaks of the need for faith, but not religion. Religion is a system, an institution.

claims, it would be a disaster, for it would shut down the structure of time and history, removing hope, desire and expectation. There would no longer be any future… or mystery. An interesting point.

AN ETHICAL QUESTION

In *Faith and Knowledge*, Derrida explores themes of religion, sacrifice,

Above and left: Auschwitz, Poland. How can we forgive the unforgivable?

prayer and pardon. Religion has so many levels, influences, power struggles and plays of meaning. Is faith ever simple? He ends with the question of how pardon is possible after the Holocaust: 'The victim will always be a victim, moreover shedding any ability to see the most basic and elementary possibility of envisaging a virtual pardoning of the unpardonable.' What can faith mean in the face of atrocity?

It is impossible to define Derrida's views, and they seem to be very private. He leaves open the possibility of God, but there is no super language to speak to God in, or in which to receive messages from God – just our language. Is that enough?

Sometimes, he seems to use the word 'God' as a cipher for mystery, that which cannot be expressed, and 'the Other'.

Deconstructing the messiah

Derrida, with his Jewish heritage, deconstructs the idea of the messiah, a coming liberator and saviour of the world. The 'messiah' is the other, the ungraspable, the love of justice; if an actual figure ever came in the flesh, he

Biblical poetry tries to evoke a sense of amazement and an overturning of the order of things when it speaks of the coming messiah or kingdom of God (e.g. Isaiah 11:6–9), which stretches concepts to breaking point. On this side of the end, we cannot imagine a completion… but on the other side?

Hints of the Beyond After All

Human language can be stretched far enough to catch glimpses of the sublime and the transcendent.

Perhaps human beings can perceive glimpses and hints, suggestions of the beyond that we can only convey partially in symbol and metaphor. We need to start with the mystery of life and the depths within it: the ungraspable, the other, the undecidable. After all, the word 'doctrine' is from the Greek word *dokeo*: 'it appears or seems to be'.

Buddhist thought speaks of symbols as rafts sailing upon the sea of mystery. Buddhism works playfully with space and emptiness to suggest mystery. Barthes felt at home in aspects of Japanese culture; to him, it was a land full of empty signs, which signified everything. It has been noted that the aphorisms of some Zen masters are akin to the unsettling prodding of postmodernism.

Negative theology

If there is a God who has revealed himself/herself/itself, then that revelation must be mediated through human words and intuitions. There can be no pure revelation. Divine speak would be over the heads of

Because he may well be loved, but not thought. By love he can be caught and held, but by thinking never.

THE CLOUD OF UNKNOWING,
A MEDIEVAL MYSTICAL TEXT

Ideas are like rafts that carry us along the flow of life.

Silence is not empty.

EMPTINESS AND CLINGING

Western Buddhist Stephen Batchelor compares Buddhist sayings with postmodernism. He notes that an ancient Buddhist text by the sage Nagarjuna (c. 2nd century CE) speaks about emptiness and letting go of fixations. We must always be moving on, not clinging to opinions but being open. There is also that which is 'unfixatable by fixations', or 'incommunicable'. These sayings form a kind of set of postmodern koans. The koan is a short, pithy saying or rhyme that makes you think. It is teasing and suggestive. This non-linear thinking of the East is the forgotten aspect of thought that deconstruction and *différance* try to open up in the West.

mere mortals. Thomas Aquinas, the learned philosopher and theologian of the Middle Ages, once had a glimpse of the glory of God. He trembled, and said that all the long and wise words he had written were as straw!

Nonetheless, Aquinas argued that human words were 'adequate' to convey the hints of divine truth. Revelation is possible in a mediated sense.

Christian theology sometimes uses the apophatic tradition or the negative way. What we cannot say is as important as what we can say about God. It is a necessary corrective. God could never be grasped; he/she/it would always be beyond and ahead of us, mysterious.

Is this not the essence of deconstruction and *différance*? Leaving open the door…

Making Room for the Sublime

Avant-garde poetry, abstract art and a sense of mystery can open up our perceptions to the sublime and might awaken faith.

Lyotard argued for the abandonment of metanarratives, but he did allow a chink of light for the beyond to shine through. He wrote about experience of the sublime, that which is beyond words and form, a kind of prelinguistic sense of awe and feeling (akin to Kristeva's semiotic state). This is part of life, and should not be ignored, denied or edited out of discourse. As it is beyond form, it is best hinted at in avant-garde writings and abstract art. It is mystery, the ineffable, and we live in its embrace. Lyotard cried out for a society that is open to both a sense of justice and the unknown.

Let us wage war on totality; let us be witnesses to the unpreventable.

JEAN-FRANÇOIS LYOTARD, *THE POSTMODERN CONDITION*

Through the looking glass

Kant believed that everything is filtered through the 'spectacles' of our senses and human discourse. He took heart, though, that only God could see things as they really were in themselves. This safeguarded

reality for him, throwing an anchor into the void. Nietzsche rejected this, arguing that we can have no access to it, but only to the world of human experience and language. The 'linguistic turn' takes us back to human discourse and this world. True, but what if we can have an indirect experience of 'things in themselves' in so far as they are mediated through our senses? (Our senses are not total fabrication and illusory hyper-reality.) Language is not a prison, but a flow of responses and signifiers. And

Belief in God can be a lifeline that safeguards reality and meaning in the flow of the semiotic. But what sort of God? God must be always ahead of us, open to the future and beyond. God must flow, like life.

We experience a sense of the sublime in nature and art.

maybe we can have an indirect experience of God too, which always contains a presence and an absence? He is here and not here at the same time. No experience or vision of the divine can be total. It is always transcendent – beyond and over the edge. To say that we cannot imagine or formulate any absolutes does not mean there are none 'out there'.

A POSTMODERN FAITH?

Christianity has never claimed to have a cast-iron, watertight, all-worked-out doctrine of things. At heart, the faith is about mystery: 'the mystery of faith', as Christian texts put it. The apostle Paul once remarked that in this life 'we see but a poor reflection', but one day we shall see 'face to face' (1 Corinthians 13:12). But what sort of God is a postmodern God?

We should be able to see metanarratives as suggestive and poetic – in this way they might come alive and be very helpful as rafts to surf the edge of reality. You can believe if you want to, but you cannot prove, for then where would faith be with no doubt? Faith needs its own *différance* to allow it to be.

The Word

Allowing for the unspeakable and the imperfect expressiveness of our words, God can be believed in and can be seen to reveal himself through words and in human lives, maybe in one life par excellence.

Religions have a mystical slant and often struggle to put their ideas into words. Some things are just unspeakable, as a saint has a vision of bliss and ecstasy. Even today, near-death experiences can result in an epiphany when people near the point of death leave their bodies briefly. The sheer beauty, aliveness, freshness and light are stumblingly put into words, but they have no illusions that these are pale reflections of what they claim to have seen. The apostle Paul relates such an experience of out-of-the body bliss in one of his epistles: 'And I know that this man – whether in the body or apart from the body I do not know, but God knows – was caught up to Paradise. He heard inexpressible things, things that man is not permitted to tell' (2 Corinthians 12:3–4).

Our words are open, rich and elastic enough to convey mysteries and wonders.

The Word made flesh
Christianity revolves around the sublime enigma and

If God speaks his Word to us, then God moves alongside his creatures graciously. Insights and truths are imparted through the medium of human speech and through intuition and enlightened thoughts. They are enough; they are enough, no matter how limited and imperfect. Thus, the Muslim can believe that a shattering vision of an angel began a prophetic ministry for Muhammad in the 7th century CE, with the command to recite words given by Allah: 'Recite in the name of your Lord who created, created man from clots of blood!' or a Jew, Moses, could receive the ten commandments in a mystical encounter. They are ordinary, human words, but they could convey the divine. Pure divinity, pure transcendence, would be incommunicable and would knock us senseless. It would be like being blasted by blinding light.

Can mystery blaze through a man's eyes, and wonder echo from his life? *Resurrection* by Piero della Francesca (1415–92), in San Sepolcro, Tuscany, Italy.

mystery of God made human, the incarnation. Jesus is seen as housing the presence of God more than any other human being, for God chose to 'tabernacle', or make his home, in him. Jesus is called 'the Word', a word that is spoken

In the beginning was the Word, and the Word was with God, and the Word was God... The Word became flesh and lived for a while among us. We have seen his glory, the glory of the one and only [Son], who came from the Father, full of grace and truth.

JOHN 1:1, 14

This really is the beyond in the midst, God under the surface, revelation committed to the semiotic stream. Believers can find their faith within our worlds of discourse, hinting, pointing beyond, but never stepping out of our skins.

to humanity in our language, but more profoundly so than abstract ideas, marks on paper or spoken messages. This Word comes through flesh and blood, in man's life, revelation through a heartbeat and a touch of love.

The Mystery of the Trinity

One aspect of classical Christian doctrine, God as a holy Trinity, leads us to the edge of reality and the mystery of the unspeakable, but also the wonder of relationship and alterity.

The Trinity, a term meaning tri-unity, three-in-one, is one of the enigmas of Christian theology. God is said to be Father, Son and Holy Spirit. Preachers struggle to find ways of explaining this, and turn to everyday examples from nature – the three-leafed shamrock, beloved as a visual aid by Patrick of Ireland; the nature of H_2O as water, steam and ice; the equilateral triangle. But what does it mean to declare that God is a Trinity?

The difficulty with the above illustrations is that they are talking about impersonal things. Objects are relatively easy to divide into three sections, but a personal being is not.

If a shamrock can be seen as three-in-one, does it help us to understand God as the Trinity?

the work of God revealed in Jesus Christ; the Spirit is God at work within us.

God is therefore beyond, alongside and within, or creator, redeemer and sanctifier (one who makes us holy).

There is some truth in these models but they fall short of the fullness of the

Modes of being

Some try to reduce the persons of the Trinity to mere aspects of divinity, modes of being or of operation. Thus, God as Father is the creator; the Son is

Eastern Orthodoxy uses the icon of three angels to suggest the Trinity. It is about relationship, not three separate entities. *The Holy Trinity*, 1411.

Without God's trinity,
thinking difference is in danger
of running into thinking duality,
for without relationships of love
difference has no chance of being
celebrated, let alone established.

GAVIN D'COSTA,
SEXING THE TRINITY

traditional Christian doctrine of the Trinity. This states that God is eternally threefold in his very nature, and not just in his operations in the cosmos. This is where it all gets rather complex.

Ultimate relationships

Here we are skating at the edge of reality, dabbling on the thin ice of the limitations of our words. 'Person' when applied to the Trinity is specialized. This does not mean a separate entity or body, like an organizing team of three, but relations, distinct aspects of the whole. Theologians play with words, speaking of three persons and one substance. There is a relationship within God. This is stretching words and concepts; C.S. Lewis stated that God is not less than personal, but is 'beyond personality' in our limited, human terms.

These stretching, straining words are trying to catch the merest glimpse and hint of a divine insight. The doctrine of the Trinity reminds us that existence is relational and societal. We are all interlinked and dependent on everything else. The faith asserts a relational grounding to reality, not a static, metaphysical nature. The ground of our being is a relationship; speaking of transcendence is thus an affirmation of alterity, of the other. While rational discourse finds itself banging its head against a conceptual brick wall when looking at the Trinity, non-linear, expressive methods find a more congenial ground. An old doctrine might live again in the light of postmodernism.

Summing up

Postmodernism opens up language to the non-rational and mystery. The poetic and the sublime speak of depth, exploring the mystery of alterity – of the other – and of the gift of existence. While grand narratives are seen as imperfect and socially conditioned, they contain important insights. God, for example, can be believed in, so long as we perceive God in and through our experiences and our language. There is no stepping out of the world to see the divine in the raw.

THE FUTURE?

To return to our beginning, postmodernism means 'beyond the now'; something is always shifting, never static, anti-foundational. Going 'beyond the now' is like trying to see the horizon, screwing up your eyes to catch a glimpse, a hint – was it a mirage?

Perhaps this state of play (and those words are chosen deliberately) is in transit itself, a transient epoch of thought that will all settle down in time. Commentators sometimes suggest that postmodernism is an interim movement, on the cusp, as it were. It has been thrown up by the massive social and technological changes after the Second World War,

Gazing into the horizon is like trying to see beyond the now.

and the rebuilding not only of nations, but of a world. It is a product (at least partially) of multinational capitalism with its necessary clash of styles and the shrinking of the globe in terms of communication. How patterns of thought will develop will depend upon future economic trends.

Perhaps the whirlwind of ideas, images and changes will calm down. It is like being swept off our feet in a wild dance. The music will fade, and we will cling to our partners in a feverish sweat, swaying in the breeze and craving the quiet of the night. But what about the genie effect?

Contents

Postmodernism… has come to represent a ragbag of objections, accusations, parodies, and satires of traditional philosophical concerns and pretensions. It is largely negative, rarely positive, the celebration of an ending, but not clearly the marking of anything new.

ROBERT C. SOLOMON AND
KATHLEEN M. HIGGINS,
A SHORT HISTORY OF PHILOSOPHY

The Genie and the Lamp

We are now aware that each age is ironically self-aware of itself, its influences and its limitations. This changes everything.

In a sense, the genie has been let out of the lamp and there is no getting it back in. Once we have made a wish, there is no going back. Postmodernism has opened our eyes to the limitations and the cultural influences of each era in the arts, science and philosophy. We are ironically self-aware, and that cannot be switched off. It is like the colonial native who sees the need for liberty and the slave who dreams of emancipation. Once ideas are in our heads, there is no turning back…

This fact cannot be stressed enough. Never before has humanity been so self-aware of the cultural limitations of our thought. Every retro/nostalgic style and programme on TV brings this to mind. We constantly revisit the past and reinvent it to a

Pop art began in the mid-1950s, and took inspiration from modern popular culture, drawing on familiar images from advertising, comic strips, cinema and television.

THE EMPEROR'S NEW CLOTHES?

It is possible to become shallow and despairing of where things are going. The pop art of the 1960s has given way to conceptual art, with controversial exhibitions at major galleries in the late 20th and early 21st centuries. Tracey Emin's unmade bed and Damien Hirst's sawn-up cattle floating in preserving fluids push the boundaries of what is to be considered as 'art'. Emin throws the everyday back at us as part of a performance, and Hirst broods over the very carnality of our lives; we are hunks of meat walking. Others see little or no skill in all of this, and fear that we are being deluded. Our obsession with style, image and change perhaps bemoans an emptiness, an illusion of sophistication when we have nothing more to say.

The postmodern philosophers we have surveyed take us further than this; they seek profundities even if they do not always know how to approach them, and they certainly have values. Even Baudrillard wants us to get back to reality, before the mass-marketing media turn everything into a product and therefore an illusion.

... aesthetic production today has become integrated into commodity production generally.

FREDRIC JAMESON,
POSTMODERNISM, OR, THE CULTURAL LOGIC OF LATE CAPITALISM

degree for contemporary purposes. Andy Warhol, for example, took images from popular culture and immortalized them on large screen prints. He sometimes mixed images and styles, tongue in cheek. He revisited Leonardo da Vinci's *The Last Supper*, turning some of the images upside down. It may not have been possible some time ago to have made

programmes that trawl through a decade, as with the 1970s or 80s, looking at fashion, news, music and so on. The blinkers are off.

Naturally, we cannot possibly be completely self-consciously aware of our present limitations and influences this close to them. Yet we know that they are there, even if we cannot name all of them. Postmodernism is a fundamental paradigm shift – a change in the way we see things – that will not leave us alone.

Spectres of the Gods

Postmodernism is not about a total and radical relativism as it is often feared. Ancient ideas of stability and depth, of belief and hope cannot be so easily jettisoned from human consciousness.

The fear of the postmodern lies in the abandonment of any centre and stability, and therefore purpose, belief and value. Baudrillard said, 'The gods have been chased away. Their spectres hover over the deserts of postmodernism' (*Fragments: Cool Memories*). Baudrillard's talk of spectres should make us sit up and listen: *spectralité* is a powerful postmodern concept. Just as Derrida reminds us that Marx is not dead and buried conceptually, so the spirits come back to haunt us. Human beings cannot live without belief, faith or trust in some form. Society is formed by trust between individuals, and the human spirit has profound depths. We ignore such depths at our peril, and we transgress value at huge cost. The gods haunt us; they will not be banished.

Reconciliation
Roger Scruton castigates the postmodernists for not going far enough beyond criticizing

the structures, and makes intriguing references to reconciliation and forgiveness. There is a sense in which postmodernists have gone hurtling down the street, tearing down the barricades, but now they are stopping, rather out of breath, and are looking around. Dare they slow down? Dare they stop and rethink?

There is a need to reconcile the past and the present, and to be free to move 'beyond the now'. Let us recall that Derrida

> ... *revenge is permitted against the society from which you feel excluded and against the Father who created it. If you have reached the stage of repudiation, and are unable to advance beyond it to the reconciliation and forgiveness, which are the signs of moral maturity, then the temptation of the liberator is irresistible. 'Ruin the sacred truths,' as Marvel said; pull down the order that surrounds you; not only do you affirm yourself against it, you also liberate your fellows and will be awarded their admiring love.*
>
> ROGER SCRUTON,
> *MODERN PHILOSOPHY –*
> *AN INTRODUCTION AND SURVEY*

Are the gods really dead? They still haunt us with the reminder that we have spirit, depth and a quest for meaning. *Poseidon*, from the 2nd century BCE.

does not own the name 'postmodernist'; he prefers to see himself as enlightened about the Enlightenment, realizing its limitations and dogmas. He certainly does not wish to forsake reason or moral values. Others are speaking of 'critical realism' as the more sober philosophy 'after postmodernism', aware of its limitations and cultural influences, but also aware that there is a real world out there. It has also been pointed out that the international ecological crisis of global warming, and the more localized UK problem of foot-and-mouth disease, has galvanized belief in the scientific project to rise up and find solutions. Its grand march is far from over and its grand narrative brings hope.

Some say we are moving 'into the blue', meaning a sense of spirituality and feeling that will characterize the 21st century. (Traditionally, the colour blue is used for sky and thus for heaven, and it is a symbol of a more spiritual age – just as green is of ecological awareness.) Leave the door open to allow some of the old ways to return.

Do Not Be Afraid

We can see an example of reconciliation between scepticism and old ideas with 20th-century reactions to the philosophy of Hegel.

Hegel's sweeping scheme, with its grand narrative of emancipation and the triumph of spirit and reason, falls exactly into the criticism of metanarratives that Lyotard brings to bear. Hegel assumes too much power; no human being can stand outside the world and see how it works. All our knowledge, all epistemology, is limited and contingent. There are no absolute truths any more, or not in human language anyway. Perhaps our *épistèmes*, our

The master and the slave

In a myth of his own creation, Hegel comments that two individuals struggle for self-recognition. One is dominant and the other takes on the role of the slave. The master is dependent upon the slave's labour, and therefore is not really free. Gradually, the slave gains dignity and self-esteem through his labour, and seeks freedom again. Meanwhile, the master has grown decadent and incapable of control by any creative and intelligent means.

The obvious parallel is the process of development in a colonized nation. This myth formed a parable of historical struggle within communities, and the quest for a more egalitarian, enlightened society. It has inspired political thinkers such as Marx, and existentialists such as Sartre, with its desire for emancipation and freedom.

So, even an arch-absolutist like Hegel can still teach us a thing or two.

Philosopher Georg Wilhelm Friedrich Hegel.

The owners of the tobacco plantation shown in this 17th-century engraving are dependent on slave labour. According to Hegel's myth, the slaves' work gives them the self-esteem to seek their own freedom, while the master has essentially lost control through decadence.

modes or thought systems, are somewhat imaginative and poetic, more so than was ever thought or admitted. As such, they capture valid insights and can be used.

Hegel rethought

Just so, Hegel can be dusted off. Alexandre Kojève (1902–68) was a Russian émigré who taught at the École Pratique des Hautes Études between 1933 and 1939. His lectures and writings have influenced postmodern thinkers. He argued that we need contemporary (and therefore creative/imaginative) interpretations of Hegel with his scheme for viewing the

> *It may be that life can only be understood backwards, but it has to be lived forwards.*
>
> SØREN KIERKEGAARD, *THE SICKNESS UNTO DEATH*

sweep of the past in the light of the present, and of openness to the future. How should we deal with Hegel's ideas about the absolute? Hegel believed that the human mind/spirit could eventually attain knowledge of the absolute. Kojève reinterpreted this as the never-ending project of philosophy to constantly rethink things. There would be no finite end to the project; it was set against an infinite horizon. The absolute was transmuted into the infinite, and we are always moving along that road. This freed the future to be unpredicatable and unexpected, rather than determined by the past, as Hegel had taught.

Kojève was particularly concerned with a passage in Hegel's *Phenomenology*, which dealt with the master and the slave. In this he saw the violent struggle for emancipation that runs right through history. If we forget this dynamic, we might be condemned to repeat it again and again.

A Postmodern Creed

By way of a conclusion, trying to sum up all the many ideas, arguments and teasing paradoxes in this book on postmodernism, a non-discursive ending has been arranged, written in the form of a creed.

*B*e open.
Be open to life.
Be open to ideas.
Be open to love.

*Be open to the call and presence
of the other.*
You are not alone, sealed up, a living prison cell. You are open at the edges to other people. We find ourselves in giving up something to the other. This is true freedom.

Appreciate the gift.
The life that flows through you and that you flow within is a gift. Be thankful for what is given to you. This world is not a consumer paradise, a green and blue shopping mall, that we can rape and pillage as we wish. Life is more than commodities.

The illusion of control is always with us. We are not in command of our destiny, or this planet. Not really. It happens to us. Flow.

Be tolerant of others and their views.
Feel free to disagree, but always let them have space to be.

The Angel of the Flowing Light by Cecil Collins (1908–89).

Avoid doctrinaire, totalitarian systems. They hurt people. That does not mean that you cannot hold strong views, deeply valued principles and ideas. By all means do so. Feel them from the heart. Just allow others space to be too.

What we think there is might not always be the case.
Sometimes our glasses have misted over and the lenses

*A burning glass is the soul who
in her cave joins with the source
of light to set everything ablaze
that approaches her hearth.*

LUCE IRIGARAY,
SPECULUM OF THE OTHER WOMAN

distort reality. Always be open, never think it is all sewn up. You have not and cannot have all the answers. Do not try to catch the universe in your mind. It is like the boy who thought he could put the sea in a bucket! There is always more. Always.

Do not be afraid of Big Things.
When challenged and engulfed by a 'big system', take out your deconstruction tools and see it fall apart like unscrewed Meccano. Recognize the cultural influences, the power plays. Spot the slippages.

Love is.
Do not doubt that. We run on that. It is soul-forming. Love is, prior to language and all belief systems. Love is. It draws us out, on, beyond. It turns the head of Narcissus if received rightly.

Feel the mystery blowing in your face.
It is all right to be perplexed and awestruck. Be open to the unknown. There is that which we cannot represent adequately. Feel free to call that 'God' if you wish. You can believe if you want. Face the void. What is life, what are our fleeting selves, what is meaning? It is bigger than we are.

Life is not a random free-for-all.
This is so, even though there are many theories and viewpoints. What we do to others matters to them and to us. Kill a man and you kill yourself, within. We are all connected. Existence is societal. Respecting the other, the gift, involves ethics. How we act matters.

Look into your soul, into your secret place.
Feel the *chora* within, that deep, dark mystery self, full of drives and playfulness. Recognize yourself. Seek light. Connect.

Rapid Factfinder

A

abject: a state of extreme emotion and desolation beyond words. Used in the psychoanalysis of Julia Kristeva.

alterity: 'otherness', pertaining to 'the other', from the Latin *alter* for 'other', as in alter ego.

anthropic principle: we exist because the universe exists in a certain manner. Thus, we can begin to analyse it.

apophatic: the tradition of negative theology to assert mystery and the limits of human knowledge about God.

aporia: Greek for 'no passage' or 'no path'. It is a conceptual or literary cul-de-sac, a slippage of meaning. If *x* is the case, as stated, then how can *y* exist too? This shows that the author's conscious intent is not the only dialogue or set of ideas going on.

archaeologies: tracing the history of an idea or an institution to reveal its development and the influences upon it, and to dethrone its claim to power and right interpretation. This was begun by Nietzsche's genealogies and developed by Foucault.

archetypal images: Jung's idea that there are common, potent symbols across cultures that represent deep drives in our psyches.

B

binary opposition: the dualism of setting one thing against another, such as light/dark, life/death, peace/war, speech/writing.

C

Cartesian: to do with Descartes, from the Latin for his name.

Cartesian dualism: the idea that the mind and body are separable entities.

categorical imperative: Kant's dictum that some things are always right and ethical in every circumstance, no matter how many difficulties this places you in.

chora: an ancient Greek term for the state or place of creation. This was primeval chaos. Kristeva and others describe the infantile, prelinguistic self as the *chora*, where we express things without, or beyond words.

cogito: the thinking subject.

cognitive slippage: a moment in a text where meaning slips and we are aware of repressed ideas or contradictory ideas at play.

collective unconscious: Jung's term for the depths of the psyche and the links between people, societies and ages.

D

deconstruction: Derrida's method of criticizing a text or an ideology that shows both the many unconscious influences brought to bear upon it and the inherent contradictions, slippages of meaning, and repressed ideas. See also *aporia*.

deterritorialized self: the idea coined by Deleuze and Guattari whereby we are programmed by capitalist forces in society to have a certain identity and role. Desire is repressed and freedom curtailed.

dialectical method: formulated by Hegel and employed by Marx, this shows how a thesis and an antithesis can result in a synthesis.

différance: Derrida's own term from a mixture of 'differ' and 'defer'. This points out the space between words, the frame that gives contextual meaning, the deferred other meanings or ideas that are necessary to make any statement. It implies the existence of responses of 'Yes, but…'

E

écriture féminine: a literary movement in France that seeks to allow women to write as women, expressing emotions and in language that bends the normal rules of grammar. It is highly evocative and imaginative, and is concerned with the tactile and the body. The phrase 'writing the body' is sometimes used, meaning creating an awareness of bodily issues.

ego: the term coined by Freud for the conscious, rational self, which is only superficial.

ego ideal: Lacan's term for the social, symbolic order that forms an image of what we should be.

empiricism: the attempt to restrict knowledge to what can be measured and apprehended by the five senses.

end of history: Fukuyama's notion that social development has reached its zenith with the advent of liberal democracy (and therefore capitalism).

end of man: Foucault's idea that our sense of being a fixed substance is forever over as we see the social influences that help to define our sense of self in different ages. For example, psychoanalysis has swept away the Cartesian idea of the self as a solitary, thinking thing in the body.

Enlightenment: the movement from the 17th to 18th centuries that sought to use reason, observation and the scientific method to analyse the world.

***épistèmes*:** Foucault's term for systems of discourse or understanding that become foundational in different ages.

existentialism: a 20th-century philosophy that stressed that we are not fixed essences, but fluid experiences. We create a sense of self as a lifetime project.

F

foundationalism: the attempt to find solid, sure, fixed points in knowledge, whether in words, experience, thought or metaphysical beliefs.

G

genealogy: Nietzsche's term for the history of an idea or a structure, such as 'the genealogy of morals', tracing the different developments and influences through the ages.

gift: the givenness of life and our existence – the fact of the relational nature of life and the existence of others as well as the self.

golden rule: the basic idea that we should treat others as we want to be treated.

Ground of our Being: Tillich's phrase for rethinking theology. God is envisaged as more abstract, and in terms of depth, not height.

H

hyper-reality: simulated existence beyond the temporal. Events that

have long since ceased in reality can live on in repeated films.

I

id: Freud's term for the depths of the human psyche beyond the rational ego.

ideal: Lacan's idea that there are strong influences given to an infant from recent ancestors that shape the child's developing sense of identity and behaviour patterns.

ideal ego: Lacan's sense of the original ideas of self held by the developing infant; closely related to his concept of the ideal.

idealism: the 17th-century movement that stressed the innate power of reason to understand reality, rather than observation of the external world.

incarnation: the Christian doctrine that God became human in Jesus Christ.

individuation: a sense of self-identity and self-worth, becoming centred and self-confident.

J

***jouissance*:** a term meaning intense pleasure and release of energy and emotion that is beyond words.

L

language games: Wittgenstein's argument that different areas of life and disciplines utilized different rules of discourse. The emotions and rational discourse both had their own rules.

linguistic turn: the movement in the 20th century to go back to language, to realize that this was a human construction and did not simply correspond to reality 'out there'.

logical atomism: an attempt to reduce sentences to their basic ingredients, and to only allow valid meaning to things that had clear reference to empirical objects or states.

logical positivism: the belief that meaning only applies to rational, empirical matters. Anything else is obscurantist nonsense.

logocentrism: Derrida's idea that the attempt to fix meaning and to have metaphysical foundations was to centre on the *logos* – reason – at the expense of other forms of discourse.

M

messianicity: Derrida's deconstruction of the messianic to stress the constant need for openness to the other, and to new, creative and just ideas. He would almost say that if the messiah came, refuse to believe in him, for life cannot ever be complete and perfect. The journey must always go on.

metanarratives: grand narratives, 'big theories of everything', which sum up history, life, economics or philosophy (hence Darwinism, Marxism, Christianity). The term was used widely by Lyotard.

mirror stage: the stage in Lacan's psychology whereby the infant relates to an image of self that is the foundation of its future development. This comes from its surroundings and family.

modernism: the late 19th and early 20th-century movement that sought to promote both technological advance and experimental forms of art and expression. It was inherently optimistic and followed a belief in progress.

N

narcissism: Freudian term referring to self-love and arrested infantile development. It comes from the Greek myth of Narcissus, who fell in love with his own reflection.

negative theology: theologians stress what cannot be said about God to enhance God's transcendence and mystery.

noumena: Kant's term for the world as it is in itself, unlike our understanding of it.

O

Oedipal: Freud's idea of a stage of human development. This was based upon the Greek myth of Oedipus, who killed his father. The theory goes that, in a quest for self-identity, the male seeks to overthrow the father and the female realizes that she is different and lacks something, namely a penis. She turns inwards and seeks self-identity through childbearing.

other: any other sentient being, animal, human or God; we are primarily relational beings and define ourselves against the other.

P

paradigm shift: a major shift in the way that something is understood, whether religion, economics or science.

penis envy: Freudian theory that women have a sense of lack because they do not have a penis. Lacan developed this in terms of discourse and the world of the symbolic. The phallus was an archetypal symbol. Men experience a separation from the mother and an entrance into the world of rational, objective discourse. Women experienced a separation from this.

pharmakon: From the word from which we derive 'pharmacy'. It has a dual meaning in ancient texts as cure or as poison. Derrida uses it in this double-edged, undecidable manner to show how writing and speech are not in primary and secondary positions.

phenomena: Kant's term for the world as it is interpreted in our experience, as through a pair of spectacles.

phenomenology: an early form of existentialism pioneered by Husserl and then Heidegger. It is concerned with experience, this being the only thing that is present to us in any certainty. We live in being; we make abstract ideas about it.

postfeminism: an attempt to avoid the radical extremes of early feminism that sought separation from men and attempted androgyny. Postfeminists affirm difference between the sexes as a form of essential, given alterity that is creative and ethical.

post-structuralism: the movement that seeks to question the work of Saussure in linguistics and Lévi-Strauss in anthropology. Things cannot be analysed and regulated in the precise ways these men have suggested. A number of thinkers who are dubbed 'postmodernist' have only owned the epithet 'post-structuralist'.

pre-Oedipal: Freud's idea of the early stages of childhood before there is a real sense of separation and contest with the father.

presence: a key idea in logocentric, metaphysical thinking. Here, we can be really present to ourselves, our experiences and the external world. Postmodernists claim that

all our experiences are interpreted. There is no seeing reality in the raw in any sense.

pre-Socratics: the Greek philosophers who were born before Socrates (470–399 BCE). They were early examples of logical thinkers. Some were materialistic and some mystical. They could be poetic and imaginative, some belonging to religious cults.

Psych et po: French feminist group standing for *psychanalyse et politique*. This group affirmed the masculine and the feminine, and recognized an essential otherness between the sexes.

R

real: Lacan's term for the aspects of experience and perception that cannot be systematized in rational discourse or the realm of the symbolic.

Renaissance: the rebirth of learning that revived classical knowledge in the late Middle Ages.

S

Scholastics: the medieval doctors of the church, such as Thomas Aquinas, who followed the ancient philosophy of Aristotle as a guide to life alongside the scriptures.

seduction techniques: Baudrillard's way of subverting ideas and structures by teasing out conflicts and contradictions, and setting contrary symbols and ideas alongside each other. This can be close to the work of the satirist, bringing out falsity and lack.

semiotic: Kristeva's term for the pre-Oedipal infant who has not developed language and its symbolic terms of reference.

semiotic stream: the flow of words and the play of signifiers in a text or discourse.

semiotics: the study of the structure of language.

shadow: Jung's archetypal image for the repressed, negative forces within us.

simulacrum: a term used by Baudrillard for the virtual reality that signs can take on as they overtake reality and assume a life of their own.

slave ethic: Nietzsche's analysis of a corrupted form of Christian ethics whereby the weak are praised. Lack, failure and poverty are elevated. He contrasts this with the noble ethic of strength, courage and daring.

SOS Racisme: a French anti-racism movement.

spectralité: the idea that spectres, ghosts, are forces and ideas that will not lie down and stay dead. They haunt us, beckoning us to listen to their wisdom. Derrida writes of Marxism in this light, and postmodernism sometimes talks of religion and God in this way.

structuralism: the attempt to discern deep structures to human language that cross cultures, and to apply this to sociology, showing common ideas and organizational patterns across the world. The former method is associated with Saussure, and the latter method with Lévi-Strauss.

superego: Freud's term for the censor or filter mechanism that keeps hurtful memories and thoughts from waking consciousness (the ego).

supplement: Derrida's term for the way that something or someone is put in a secondary position, such as writing/speech or king/prince. The supplement actually adds something distinctive, in its own right. It can turn things around and subvert the usual order.

symbolic realm: Lacan's term for the social world of discourse and the way that individuals are formed by it and grafted into it.

T

Tel Quel: A 1970s and 80s French literary, intellectual journal run by a group of thinkers that included a number of postmodernists.

trace: the trace of things referred to by a word or sign in a discourse, but not always explicitly present. Derrida points out that everything in a text relates to another sign in the text, and only indirectly to actual things 'out there'. Discourses are huge games with constant cross references.

Trinity: the Christian doctrine that God is three persons in one substance.

U

Übermensch: the Superman or Overman as coined by Nietzsche: the self-determined, strong, noble individual.

ultimate reality/concern: Tillich's terms for God or transcendence that seek to locate theological discourse within ordinary human experience, rather than a particular belief system. Thus, we all face questions of ultimate concern (ethics, life and death), and are faced with the question of whether life has meaning or not (ultimate reality).

uncertainty principle: Heisenberg's term for the inability of scientific observers to measure precisely two or more variables simultaneously, such as the momentum and position of an electron.

unconscious: the deep level of the mind below conscious thoughts.

undecidability: categories that cannot be placed in regular binary opposites. Is a ghost alive or dead? Is the mind physical or immaterial? This is part of Derrida's strategy of undermining Western metaphysical assumptions.

universal test: Kant's method of defining a categorical imperative. If an action will always result in hurt to someone else, then it is always wrong (e.g. stealing).

V

void: a term that can mean emptiness and meaninglessness, or the flux of life in its wholeness that defies human analysis and totalizing explanations.

W

will to power: Nietzsche's term for the drive to control and master others. This affects ideologies and governments. It plagues philosophy with unconscious agendas and motives.

Word: a translation of the Greek term *logos*, which is used in Christian doctrine for the indwelling of God in Jesus Christ.

Index of Key Thinkers

Aristotle (384–322 BCE): Greek philosopher who wrote about many subjects. He thought that everything had its own *telos* or purpose for which it was made.

Roland Barthes (1915–80): French philosopher who applied Saussure's ideas to the study of literature, noting unconscious structures and also the power of the media to 'frame' truth.

Jean Baudrillard (1929–): French postmodern philosopher who is concerned with reality, the media and illusion.

Simone de Beauvoir (1908–86): Feminist writer famed for *The Second Sex*. Companion of Jean-Paul Sartre.

Hélène Cixous (1937–): French postfeminist writer and professor of English in Paris.

Gilles Deleuze (1925–95): French philosopher who sought to think in new concepts, and to imagine the possibilities of mechanical life forms rather than carbon-based ones.

Jacques Derrida (1930–): Algerian-born, post-structuralist philosopher working in Paris. He has pioneered deconstruction and criticized the whole project of Western philosophy as being 'logocentric'. His ideas of 'undecidability' show how some things do not fit into neat categories.

René Descartes (1596–1650): French philosopher who questioned the Scholastics and the foundations of medieval thought. He trusted only the *cogito* – the thinking self – and the clear and distinct ideas it could form about the external world.

Michel Foucault (1926–84): French post-structuralist thinker who followed Nietzsche in seeking the history or archaeology behind an idea. He exposed power plays and social influences in claims to truth.

Sigmund Freud (1856–1939): Austrian doctor who pioneered psychoanalysis and the interpretation of dreams.

Felix Guattari (1930–92): French philosopher who collaborated with Deleuze. Both toyed with new ways of thinking, and of seeing human history as part of a much larger and more ancient 'geology' of the world and of life.

Georg Wilhelm Friedrich Hegel (1770–1831): German philosopher who developed dialectics, whereby a thesis and antithesis becomes a synthesis. He also believed that *Geist*, or Spirit, guided history and was leading humanity to a knowledge of the absolute.

Martin Heidegger (1889–1976): German philosopher, and a pupil of Husserl. He developed phenomenology into what became known as existentialism.

David Hume (1711–76): Scottish philosopher who worked during the Enlightenment. He was sceptical about supernatural and religious claims, but also chided empiricists for basing so much on observation alone.

Edmund Husserl (1859–1938): German philosopher who taught phenomenology, and thought that only our experiences were a direct knowledge of reality.

Luce Irigaray (1932–): French postfeminist writer and analyst who stressed that sexual difference is an important basis for ethics.

Carl Gustav Jung (1875–1961): A disciple of Freud who deviated sharply from his ideas, developing his own methods of psychoanalysis. He taught that there was a collective unconscious, and that certain symbols were potent and universal.

Immanuel Kant (1724–1804): German philosopher who wrote about ethics and knowledge. He saw sense experience as a filter, a means of interpreting external reality, rather than as a totally accurate representation of it.

Søren Kierkegaard (1813–55): Danish philosopher who struggled with the relationship between faith and reason, teaching an early form of existentialism.

Alexandre Kojève (1902–68): Hungarian philosopher who settled in France and taught Foucault and Derrida. He interpreted Hegel in a daringly new way.

Julia Kristeva (1941–): Bulgarian-born, postfeminist writer and psychoanalyst resident in France since the 1960s.

Jacques Lacan (1901–81):
French psychotherapist who developed Freud's ideas, seeing language as formative for human consciousness and self-image.

Emmanuel Levinas (1906–95):
Jewish philosopher working in France who used concepts in the Hebrew Torah to tease out ideas of ethics and transcendence.

Claude Lévi-Strauss (1908–):
structural anthropologist who applied structuralist analysis to human societies.

John Locke (1632–1704):
English philosopher in the early Enlightenment who taught empiricism. He trusted only what the five senses told us about the external world.

Jean-François Lyotard (1925–99): French postmodern philosopher who argued that metanarratives were now impossible, for each age is culturally conditioned in its ideas.

Friedrich Nietzsche (1844–1900): German philosopher who questioned many received traditions and attitudes, trying to subvert morality and the idea of 'truth'.

Plato (427–347 BCE): Greek philosopher and a disciple of Socrates. He wrote down his master's teachings and developed his own ideas about the perfect world of ideals and the imperfect, changing world we live in.

Bertrand Russell (1872–1970):
English philosopher who followed a version of logical positivism known as logical atomism, breaking sentences down into their logical component parts. Again, only what was empirical was reasonable.

Jean-Paul Sartre (1905–80):
French existentialist philosopher who taught that life offered a terrifying freedom to 'be' in the face of nothingness.

Ferdinand de Saussure (1857–1913): Swiss professor of linguistics who began to describe deep structures to language. Signifiers were free-floating, being assigned to objects accidentally and randomly.

Socrates (470–399 BCE): Greek philosopher who was famous for holding dialogues rather than writing anything down. An honest seeker after truth, a radical thinker who challenged convention and trusted reason and conscience.

Ludwig Wittgenstein (1889–1951): Austrian philosopher who settled in Cambridge, England, and began as a logical positivist, but broke away from these confines later. He taught that language used a variety of 'games' to cover different types of expression.

Picture
Acknowledgments

AKG Berlin: 9–10, 24, 25, 26, 27 (top), 27 (bottom), 28–29, 48–49, 62, 67, 68–69, 81, 86, 89, 90, 97, 98–99, 101, 102 (top), 102 (bottom), 109, 120, 128–29, 132, 137, 141, 142 (bottom), 148.

Ann Ronan Picture Library: 10, 12, 14–15, 32, 40, 44–45, 87, 100, 115, 130, 150, 151.

Art Directors and Trip: 3 (J. Okwesa), 7 (J. Stanley), 30–31, 46–47 (J. Greenberg), 51 (J. Okwesa), 76–77 (H. Roberts).

Collection Corbis Kipa: 73.

Digital Vision: 2, 43, 52, 57, 63, 75 (bottom), 78–79, 118, 127, 133, 136, 139.

Gamma: 35 (Panapress [bottom]), 42 (Françoise Viard), 59 (Bill Greenblatt/UPI [top]), 75 (Frederic Reglain [top]), 91 (Sion Touhig/FSP), 113 (Eslami-Rad), 122 (Louis Monier), 134, 135 (Semeniako).

ImageState: 2, 3, 5, 20, 21, 22–23, 23, 37, 55, 64–65, 72–73, 82, 92–93, 95, 116–17, 126, 130–31, 138, 144–45.

NASA: 38–39.

Skjoldphotographs: 83.

Tate Gallery, London: 152.

Topfoto/UPPA: 50, 90.

Topham: 4 (Empics), 35 (Keystone [top]), 61 (Photri), 66 (Fotomas), 84–85 (ImageWorks), 104–105 (Empics), 123 (PressNet).

TophamPicturepoint: cover, 13, 16–17, 19, 33, 59 (bottom), 70, 106, 110–11, 124–25, 146–47.